THE KNICKS

THE KNICKS

RED HOLZMAN

with Leonard Lewin

With photographs by George Kalinsky

DODD, MEAD & COMPANY
NEW YORK

ISBN 0-396-06342-X

Library of Congress Catalog Card Number: 76-150166

Printed in the United States of America
by The Cornwall Press, Inc., Cornwall, N. Y.

For Selma, Gail and Eddie

Illustrations

Photographs by George Kalinsky except where otherwise indicated

1

"Hey, sit down. It's not over yet." I was screaming at the players.

Bill Hosket was jumping wildly near the sideline. Donnie May had drifted almost onto the court and had both arms extended into the air. There was bedlam in the Garden.

I tried my best to control things. Walt Frazier had the ball and was dribbling. I glanced at the clock. There were nineteen seconds to go. There was no way Los Angeles could win but the ball game was not over and I didn't want the players on the floor.

I knew if they got out there, the fans would follow and we would all be swallowed up. I wanted a square shot at crossing the court before the crowd could get at us. I cautioned May and Hosket and the others near me to cool it until the buzzer sounded.

Frazier passed the ball to Dick Barnett and he hit with a jumper. Now the Knicks were ahead, 113–97, with twelve seconds remaining, and the players were uncontrollable. Bill Bradley was dancing on the court as the dam of his emotion finally broke.

There was frenzy. Still it wasn't over. Jerry West had

two foul shots. He stepped to the line and made them both. A real champion. Two useless free throws, yet he calmly made them. I felt sorry for him. All those years of trying to win a championship and now this, another defeat.

Dave DeBusschere had the ball. Nine seconds to go. I got ready. I held my arms out to restrain the players, but I sneaked closer to the sideline. I watched the clock and DeBusschere. He was eating up the seconds and I was getting ready for a running start to the dressing room. I saw the hand creeping to the final second and the buzzer went off with DeBusschere still dribbling.

I took off. I grabbed the pockets of my jacket as I ran. It was an instinctive reaction that keeps the change from flying. I didn't want to stop and have to pick up a few dimes and quarters and confront the wave of humanity that was coming out of the stands. I was halfway across the floor when I said to myself: "Willis, where's Willis? Oh, my gosh, I left him back there." I risked a glance without breaking stride. I couldn't see him. I kept going. The television lights lit up the area leading to the dressing room and I hurried past them.

I wanted to get to the dressing room and have a few words with the players but that was hopeless. Television had taken over the Rangers' room, which is adjacent to the one the Knicks use. The press and radio had confiscated our dressing room. They were in there before the players. I had seen things like this on television. I expected to be drowned in a shower of champagne.

There was some yelling and some pushing. I know there was pushing because I was doing it. I was trying to reach the players and shake a few hands. I didn't see any champagne. There was beer, though. Frazier had a bottle. So did Bradley and DeBusschere and Mike Riordan.

"I need a beer, man," chirped Frazier. He went into

trainer Danny Whelan's room and dug one out of the cooler and sat on the trainer's table. The Knicks were a beer team. All year they had their beer after the ball game and there was no reason why this night should be any different than any other night.

Willis Reed was sitting near his stall and explaining how he had managed to play in pain. I was happy to see he had made it through the mob scene outside. He was holding a bottle of beer as the press and radio jammed around him. There were pocket press conferences going on everywhere. Dick Barnett was in his quiet corner, as usual. Bradley had a foot on the stool in front of his locker. Cazzie Russell was bouncing around and grinning. Frazier and DeBusschere were in the trainer's room. Dave Stallworth was off in his little corner exposing the gold star in his upper front tooth with huge smiles.

I looked around. There was excitement and chatter but nothing like the madness I had seen in other championship dressing rooms on television. Pretty soon the champagne bottles began replacing some beer bottles in the hands of the players. The television people wanted more champagne poured. It wasn't exciting enough. Someone complied by showering Howard Cosell, on camera. Vintage? Knicks 1969-70, I assume.

"It's all over, Willis," DeBusschere screamed at the captain. "Come here, man. Let me talk to you for a second." Willis got up and walked over. DeBusschere threw his arms around Reed and kissed him. "I thought these guys were great men," grinned Barnett as he watched DeBusschere and Reed embrace, "but now I'm beginning to have my doubts."

I figured I had better get to my little office. No one was going to throw me in the shower with my clothes on. No one had carried me off the field of triumph as I had seen them do with Vince Lombardi after the Green Bay Packers

3

had won a championship. No one even bothered to ask me if I wanted any champagne when they began passing it around.

"It was the world to me to see a guy with guts just come back and play—that big fellow," said Stallworth, pointing to Reed. Imagine Stallworth saying that. He had come back from a heart attack and he was talking about the courage of someone else. It made me feel good.

I passed Bradley on the way to my office which is between the Knicks' and Rangers' dressing rooms. "Nice going, Bill," I ad-libbed. He gave me one of his patented Princeton-and-Oxford smiles and nods. I dropped into my seat behind the desk. Members of the press stopped by to say a few words and ask some questions. Not many. I preferred it that way.

The players had won the championship and they deserved all the attention. I was content to sip my beer and relax a little. It had been a long season. There had been ten exhibition games and eighty-two regular season games and then seven playoff games with Baltimore and five with Milwaukee and now seven with Los Angeles. A guy deserved a quiet beer after that.

Outside, in the dressing room, DeBusschere suddenly got a thought. "Say," he said, "has anyone gotten the coach yet?" He was asking Hosket because Bill had become the self-appointed pourer of champagne over everyone's head. Hosket shot the eyes out of the bottle. He didn't miss anyone. He got players and reporters and cameramen.

Hosket confessed that he had overlooked the coach. "Let's get him," said DeBusschere, grabbing a fresh bottle. So did May and Riordan. They walked into my office. I could sense something was going to happen by the silly little grins on their faces.

"Hya, coach," said DeBusschere, trying to fake me out

with some conversation. They gave it to me. Over my head, into my eyes, down my face and onto my clothes the champagne cascaded. They emptied three bottles on me. Me, Red Holzman, the kid from Brooklyn, getting a bath in imported champagne. Only in America.

This was more like it. This I had seen on television. I enjoyed it. So it shouldn't be a total loss, I caught some of the champagne with my tongue as it rolled down my face and swallowed. It tasted almost as good as the championship the Knicks had just won for the first time in their history. Let me tell you, twenty-four years can be a long time to suffer.

Frazier, for example, was only one when the 1946 Knicks played their first game in the Basketball Association of America. So was Riordan. Old man Barnett was ten, Reed was four, Bradley was three, Cazzie was two and Hosket had not been born yet. Many of the people who saw the Knicks finally win it all had been there from the beginning. They could tell better than I what a long haul it had been until it happened.

This was a night to remember. Even for me. I had been on a championship team before but it was nothing like this. Ironically, when I was playing for the Rochester Royals, we beat the Knicks in the seventh game for the 1950-51 title. We kind of spoiled the champagne party they had planned to celebrate their first championship.

We had taken the first three games and they won the next three. The final game was on our court. Ned Irish brought the Knicks to Rochester in a chartered plane, which he had stocked with champagne. The team was flying right back after the game and he figured he would have the stuff handy for a victory celebration—just in case.

The Knicks came close. They led late in the game. But it was tough beating us on our floor. We had some pretty good ballplayers. Bob Davies, Bobby Wanzer, Pep Saul and I handled the backcourt, and we had rugged size in Arnie Risen, Jack Coleman and Arnie Johnson. We had another edge—the court, itself. There was very little room at either end and you would get pretty banged up running into the walls if you didn't know how to handle the bounces.

I'll say this, the Knicks did very well. They were a smart team and well coached by Joe Lapchick. Anytime you beat Harry Gallatin, Sweetwater Clifton, Ernie Vandeweghe, Vince Boryla, Carl Braun and Dick McGuire, you knew you had accomplished something. We did it by four points (79–75) in the final game, and we had the victory champagne in the dressing room.

The Knicks had their champagne on the plane going home. I'm sure, however, it never tastes so good in defeat. Irish wanted his players to have it, anyway. He is first class about things like that. He appreciated how far they had gone and how hard they had worked and they had won something. So the plane took off and the corks popped.

Irish hovered around the stuff as unofficial wine steward. He supervised the pouring. Players and reporters wandered back and forth to the rear of the plane for refills. Lapchick got up for another glass and plopped back in his seat just in time to see the pilot walk back for some champagne. A few seconds later, Lapchick did a double take. Could it be? It was. The copilot had walked by to join the pilot in the rear.

"Who the hell is flying the plane?" asked Joe.

"I dunno," said a scared guy next to him.

"Let's go and see," suggested Lapchick.

So the two got up and walked toward the front hoping to find someone at the controls. They were afraid to think that the plane was on automatic pilot.

They got to the cockpit and peeked in. "Hya, coach,"

said the guy at the controls. The voice was familiar. So was the face when it turned for a second. It was Bud Palmer, the Bill Bradley of his day. Palmer, a Princeton star, had played with the original Knicks and had retired after three seasons. Now he was accompanying the team as a radio man. He was doing the color on the broadcasts.

And what was Palmer doing at the controls of the plane? Well, Bud had done some flying in the Navy, so he asked the pilot if he could handle the ship. The pilot got up and decided he would go back for some champagne as long as the copilot was up there. Then the copilot suggested he would like some champagne, so Palmer convinced him to go on back for a few seconds because the plane was in good hands.

Now, nineteen years later, Ned Irish was providing victory champagne and I was swallowing some. Life is full of strange little bounces like that. At least my life has been full of them. I have experienced so many, not very much surprises me anymore. It is amazing how important it is to be in the right place at the right time.

I thought of that as I listened to the excitement in the dressing room and when the reporters came in to ask me questions. They expect me to say something profound. I try and tell them I'm not a genius. They don't want to hear that. They want me to worry about things that people seem to worry about and get excited about things that people seem to get excited about.

My father used to say: "If we live, we'll go Saturday. If not, we'll go Sunday." It was his way of telling us that you shouldn't worry over things you can't control. When I say things like that to the newspapermen, they think I'm kidding. They laugh and pretty soon they give up in disgust because I don't tell them what they would like to hear.

What am I going to tell them? That I dreamed up some

psychological idea that inspired Willis Reed beyond the normal threshold of pain? Or gave Walt Frazier the secret of how to steal the ball from Jerry West? Or played defense for Bill Bradley and Dave DeBusschere? Or found a serum that keeps Dick Barnett playing younger and younger? Or taught Cazzie Russell to break a team's back with his shooting?

Yes, I had worked hard to help make the Knicks a team. But so had the players. So had Ned Irish and Irving Mitchell Felt. So had Eddie Donovan before he left to take over the Buffalo Braves. So had Joe Lapchick, Carl Braun, Dick McGuire, Vince Boryla and Fuzzy Levane, the man who brought me to the Knicks in the first place. They coached the team at one time or another and they all contributed in their own way to the success that finally came on May 8, 1970.

I sat behind my desk, sipping my beer and thinking of things like that as the reporters asked questions. Soon they wandered back to the players. Then the men began moving out of the dressing room. They were splitting up to go to their own little parties. I poked my head in and saw Willis and Frazier still in there. "Nice going, fellows," I said.

Then I left to join Selma, my wife, and my daughter Gail. They were in the pressroom with a few friends from Puerto Rico who had flown up in the morning to see the game. Willie Vicens of Ponce, his cousin Pacin and Dr. Arnold Hernandez had left Puerto Rico at three in the afternoon and arrived just at game time. We had a few drinks in the Penn Plaza Club and that was about it. Gail went off with her boyfriend.

My friends said goodbye. Selma and I went to the car and headed out the Long Island Expressway for the drive home to Cedarhurst. We had made that trip maybe a thousand times. Sometimes we would stop off at the Turnpike Restaurant on Queens Boulevard to take some delicatessen sandwiches home. This night we drove straight to Cedarhurst. It was my night. No traffic on the expressway that has been described as the world's largest parking lot.

We talked about the game. We talked about Willis and Frazier. We talked about Jerry West and Elgin Baylor . . . how those poor guys are so great yet never have played on a championship team. We pulled the car into our driveway and it was good to be home. It was hard to believe it was all over and that there was no practice tomorrow.

I walked into the kitchen and poured myself a drink—Dewar's and water with a lot of ice. Selma had her customary soda. I like scotch with a lot of ice. I even drink beer over ice when I can get it. Sounds crazy but that's what I like.

I took my scotch and water and went into the den. I turned on the television and sat in my favorite easy chair. The game was on. I got home in time to see the second half of the rerun. Channel 7 had televised the game live nationally, with New York blacked out, and had programmed it later that night locally.

I saw Willis, Frazier, DeBusschere, Barnett, Bradley, Cazzie and Riordan do it all over again. I watched the final seconds tick off the NBA championship. I saw myself run across the court and head for the dressing room. I took another sip of my drink and I think I laughed a little. I had to laugh at all the twists and turns that had taken place in the making of the Knicks. As, for example, on the day I became the coach.

O
- - - - - - -
2

It was a rotten day. But I had to get up. There was a ball game with the Philadelphia 76ers in the afternoon. And there was trouble. The Knicks were not winning and there were ominous signs that Dick McGuire's days as coach were dwindling down to a precious few.

I felt badly about that for a few reasons. In the first place, I had recommended Dick for the job when Ned Irish was looking to replace Harry Gallatin. For another, I was a convenient replacement but I did not want to coach. I had a job I liked. Scouting for the Knicks was just fine with me.

Fuzzy Levane had gotten me the scouting job when he moved up to coach the Knicks in 1958. He called me one day and said Vince Boryla was giving up coaching to become the general manager. He asked if I would like the job of scouting. Good old Fuzzy. I can never repay him for the things he did for me.

We were teammates at Rochester and we became very close. Our families lived and ate together. One Thanksgiving, the girls, Selma and Kay Levane, went out and bought a turkey. It must have been about thirty-five pounds. We had one kid and the Levanes had two. Some of Fuzzy's relatives also were coming over for dinner.

The girls put the bird in the cellar because it was still three days to Thanksgiving. When they went down to retrieve it, they couldn't believe the smell. They were in panic. The stores were closed and they couldn't go to their bench for a replacement.

They held a meeting and came up with only one idea: scrub the bird. They bathed that turkey in salt, which helped a little. But it still smelled. Then another brilliant idea. They rushed to the bathroom and ran the water into the tub. They dropped the turkey in. There he was, in all his stinking splendor, floating around with his wings extended.

Selma and Kay kept scrubbing and scrubbing. They finally had enough. Their fingers were raw. They took the turkey and wiped him dry. Then they took him to the kitchen and they cooked him. He looked like any other nice, brownly cooked bird when everyone sat down to dinner. He rested in the middle of the table in all his festive majesty. Everyone dug in but Selma and Kay and the kids.

We were all so hungry, we never noticed the girls were not eating. The kids were on baby food, so they weren't having turkey, anyway. We devoured that bird. We thought it was great and said so to Selma and Kay. They never told us until years later what really had happened. I still say it was a great turkey. So does Fuzzy, by the time he gets it out.

He stutters, but only when he has plenty of time to say things, it seems. When he's on the radio or has to talk fast, it seldom happens. But when he sits around and just talks, he begins to stutter. Don't ask me why. He doesn't even know. But it's there and he laughs about it. That's the kind of guy he is.

One day, when we were playing in Rochester, we went to visit a hospital. We used to do things like that a lot of times. Les Harrison, the owner of the Royals, felt it was a nice thing to do and so did we. Fuzzy and a few of us walked into the ward and started at the first bed.

Each guy introduced himself. The patients had been told we were the Rochester Royals but they could not identify any of us. It came Fuzzy's turn. "I'm Dick Brown," he said, without missing a beat. Dick Brown? We looked at him. We couldn't say anything at the time. We didn't want to let the guy in the bed think we were pulling his leg.

"Dick Brown?" I said to Fuzzy, when I got the chance. "Where the hell did you come up with that one?" He laughed. "It's a lot easier than saying F-F-Fuzzy L-L-Levane," he explained.

Fuzzy went on to become the coach of the Milwaukee Hawks for Ben Kerner. When I got my release from Rochester, the first one to call was Fuz. He wanted me to play for him. He said he needed my experience in the backcourt.

The next thing I know, Fuzzy is out as coach and I'm it. I didn't want to take the job, but Kerner convinced me Fuz was out no matter what. So I accepted. I lasted until the team moved to St. Louis in 1957 and was out of a job, again.

My man Levane took care of that. The pay wasn't much to start, but I was back in New York where I had played high school ball at Franklin Lane and college ball for Nat Holman at City College. That was fine with Selma. Little Gail, now eleven, hardly knew she was from New York, except for the summers we spent back home. Everyone in the family was relieved, even Selma's mother.

I settled down in my scouting job and enjoyed the luxury of home life really for the first time in many years.

12

As each day passed, so did my desire ever to return to coaching. I did not like the insecurity. I liked it even less when Fuzzy was let go in 1960.

He had coached the Knicks to the playoffs in 1959. They had failed the previous three years and were to miss the next seven until they finally made it in 1967. By then Carl Braun had succeeded Fuzzy, and Eddie Donovan, Harry Gallatin, and Dick McGuire had followed in succession as coaches.

I went about my business of scouring the country for talent. Nobody bothered me and I hope I bothered nobody. Every time there was a coaching change, they looked past me. Then one day it happened. Gallatin was through. The 1965 season was on but the Garden people wanted a change because the Knicks were not doing well.

Donovan had moved upstairs to general manager when Gallatin came in, so he was part of the decision making. It was hard to get a qualified coach with the season on. Pretty soon the wheel spun to Donovan. He was asked to resume coaching but turned it down for personal reasons. Then they started to look at me.

I didn't want the job at all. I was happy with what I was doing. I couldn't refuse it if they insisted. But it never got that far because we all decided on Dick McGuire. He had done a nice job in Detroit and left there only because his family could not get adjusted. He was an all-time Knick with a great New York image.

Agreed. McGuire was to be the coach and Holzman would remain as scout. Happiness all around. It was close but I was back on the road, and Donovan was in the front office. Together, we were supplying players for the Knicks and McGuire and victory, we hoped.

Scouting and drafting are the lifeline of pro basketball. The Knicks started to do better when there was a slight change in thinking. We decided to draft the best man

13

available regardless of his position. I guess we learned the hard way. I think the turning point came with what happened in the cases of Art Heyman and Nate Thurmond. They came to the 1963 draft together and we took Heyman. It was a reasonable choice at the time.

Heyman had the qualifications. He was voted the top college player in the country at Duke University. He was a good scorer, a nice ball handler, and had a strong body. And he was from New York. So the Knicks, picking first, took Heyman, and San Francisco surprised everyone by taking Thurmond though it had Wilt Chamberlain at the time.

Eddie Gottlieb, then associated with the Warriors in an advisory capacity, explained why they chose a 6-11 center when the team really needed help in the backcourt. "When a man his (Thurmond's) size and ability is available, you can't pass him up," The Mogul said. "After all, if you have two big men, you can always trade one." That's what San Francisco did. It traded Chamberlain to Philadelphia.

I'll say this for Heyman, he was a great influence on the Knicks before he left. The first thing that happened was Richie Guerin went to Eddie Donovan and asked to be traded. Heyman was a Guerin type and had to be played, so Richie found himself sitting.

Heyman was young, and Guerin was in his eighth season with the Knicks. So Donovan looked around. Harry Gallatin came to town with the St. Louis Hawks. He had been instructed by Ben Kerner to see if he could get some backcourt help from the Knicks. The player Ben had in mind was Al Butler, a good jump shooter out of Niagara.

Gallatin went home with Guerin. What happened after that is one for the book—any book. Richie wound up replacing Harry as coach, and Gallatin came to the Knicks where Heyman still was playing—but not very much once Gallatin took over.

Artie did not like that. He had worked 2236 minutes in seventy-five games under Donovan in his rookie year. In 1964-65, his last season, Heyman played 663 minutes in fifty-five games. He was an All-America and a fierce competitor, and the bench was a stranger to him. One night, in a unique way, he let Gallatin know how he felt.

The team was coming back from Philadelphia on a bus. Heyman was in the middle organizing a card game. He had a big carboard on his lap and was looking for players. Gallatin, a cardplayer on occasion when he was with the Knicks, wandered over and suggested he might take a hand. "Go way," Heyman told his coach. "I can't play in your game, you can't play in mine."

Heyman lasted two seasons with the Knicks and gave the best he had. He drifted to San Francisco, Cincinnati, Philadelphia and then the American Basketball Association before retiring to go into the restaurant business in New York. In the meantime, the Knicks got luckier or better in the draft. Willis Reed, Bad News Barnes, Butch Komives and Em Bryant in 1964; Bill Bradley, Dave Stallworth and Dick Van Arsdale in 1965; Cazzie Russell in 1966; Walt Frazier and Mike Riordan in 1967; Don May and Bill Hosket in 1968 and John Warren in 1969.

So it was December 27, 1967, and Dick McGuire was in trouble. How did I know? It was the Christmas stretch and I usually took off to see some of the holiday tournaments. A scout can pack a lot of of valuable basketball into that week or so. "I think I'll go to Los Angeles," I told Donovan. I had my itinerary all set. I had filled in the dates on my pocket calendar.

He looked at me. He grinned a little. But there was a serious touch to his face. "I think you'd better stick around," he suggested. The Knicks were only eleven percentage points out of last place and were twelve games behind the first-place Celtics with only thirty-seven games played. I suspected the coaching situation was rather shaky.

There had been rumblings from the start of the season when the Knicks did not get off well. I had heard them. It is not an ideal situation for a coach not to win often when you have a Reed, Bradley, Cazzie and Frazier. It was even more complicated for McGuire because New York had not had a winner in so long.

I had talked over the situation many times with Selma. She was aware that the Knicks might be looking for a coach any day or any minute if things did not get radically better. We agreed that it did not look good for McGuire and could only hope it would turn his way quickly. If there had to be another coach, we felt anyone but I would be just great.

I climbed out of bed around eight o'clock and went downstairs for some juice and black coffee. "What a lousy day," I said to Selma. We chatted a little. I glanced at a paper. I don't know the exact time but the phone rang. Selma picked it up. She handed me the phone. "It's Mr. Irish," she announced.

Now what could he possibly want at this hour of the morning? The game with the 76ers was in the afternoon and I would be in my office around twelve or two hours before game time. We could talk then. But he wanted to talk now and I soon found out why.

"We'd like you to be the coach," he said. What could I say? "I don't think I'd like to do it," I replied. "Sometimes," he said, "we have to do a lot of things we don't like to do."

I could take a hint. "I have to talk to my wife," I answered. He said he would see me in the Garden. I got off the phone and started to tell Selma. She knew. She had

16

heard. We agreed it still might not happen. Maybe the Knicks would win that afternoon and go off on a wild streak and save McGuire. Maybe if they lost, and they insisted on a new coach, I could sit with them and convince them of someone else.

We got into the car and drove toward New York. We did not talk much. We were thinking. I was smoking a cigar as usual. It was cold and the windows were shut. "You're making me nauseous with that smelly cigar," said Selma. That brought me back to reality. So did the Long Island Expressway. It was ripped up and it was a pain in the neck.

But it served a purpose. It gave us something to talk about. We didn't want to talk about the coaching situation. And when you are married over twenty years, what is there to talk about other than the Long Island Expressway?

We parked the car at the Garden—the old Garden. We went up to my office on the second floor. Donovan dropped in and we talked a little; he said he would join me up in the mezzanine press box, where I always sat for the ball games. He knew how I felt. He also knew how McGuire felt. He was in the middle of a tough predicament. Nobody likes to tell a nice guy like Dick McGuire he is finished as the coach.

I know how I felt when Ben Kerner told me I was out. It was the only thing he could do because the team was losing. He had Bob Pettit and he had just moved from Milwaukee. He was struggling for his existence and had to come up with a winner for St. Louis. You expect to get fired but it hurts when it happens. It hurts your pride. You always feel you did a good job, and things would get better if they just gave you time.

Alex Hannum insists to this day he cried when he heard Kerner fired me. Can you picture that big lug crying over anything? I believe him when he says he was upset. Alex is a good-natured, sensitive human being and I had gotten him a job as a player with the Hawks. He had been dropped by Syracuse and had no place to go but home to California.

"If it wasn't for Red Holzman," Hannum has told people, "I would have quit basketball right then and there and gone into something else." I convinced Kerner that Alex could help with his muscle. Ben signed him. It was the Fuzzy Levane and Red Holzman bit all over again.

When Kerner let me go, he insisted that Slater Martin take the job. Martin, a member of the great Minneapolis Lakers team with George Mikan, Vern Mikkelsen and Jim Pollard, had come to the Hawks from the Knicks. He was traded to St. Louis for Willie Naulls and was a smart basketball player. Kerner figured he would make a good coach.

Martin thought otherwise. He didn't want to coach. Kerner persisted, and Martin coached, but not for long. He convinced Kerner he didn't want the job. "Get another coach or I go home to Texas," he told Ben. Who? "Hannum," volunteered Slater. "He's been sitting on the bench and doing the coaching while I've been playing." Hannum, who felt so badly when I was fired, wound up with my job.

That's the way it goes. A guy is a fool to worry about things like that, but it happens often. I ran into the same situation when Kerner asked me to replace Levane. When a job is open, it is open. But you just can't help feeling funny if they ask you to fill a job that has been made available because they fire a friend. I learned a lot of things from Kerner, a very, very bright man. We still have a close relationship.

Now, I dropped into the Knicks' dressing room before the game and chatted with McGuire. It was a ritual. Eddie

Donovan and I liked the idea of letting the players know we were part of the involvement. We wanted to be there, and it also was important to show the players we were interested.

We stood off at one side of the room and exchanged bits of information with Dick about the game coming up with the 76ers. I felt a little uncomfortable and so did Donovan over the situation. We tried to be nonchalant but it was difficult. We made small talk and left as soon as it was reasonable and not too conspicuous.

When I closed the door on the way out, I was rooting deep down for something good to happen for McGuire. I wasn't even sure if winning the game would help him. I didn't want the job and he did, so I could do nothing less than hope the Knicks would win and look very good doing it.

I climbed the stairs to the mezzanine and stopped for a hot dog and beer. I suddenly felt hungry. I got to my seat five minutes before game time. The mezzanine press box was a good place to watch a game in the old Garden. When you sat up there, you were rooting. Boy, how I was rooting for Dick.

It didn't help. Hal Greer and Wilt Chamberlain were too much. Donovan showed up at half time. The Knicks were losing 68–50, so I knew why he was there. "Ned wants to see you in his office," said Eddie. If Ned Irish wanted to see me, that was it.

Nothing could happen in the second half to change things. They had made up their minds. The Knicks actually went ahead, 82–81, and I was wondering what would happen if they won as I walked into Irish's office. The 76ers took care of that. They won. As soon as the final buzzer sounded, I was on my way.

I usually dropped by the dressing room after a game and then went to pick up my wife. I sent a message to

Selma that I would be delayed and she should wait in my office. I walked into Irish's office. Donovan was there.

Eddie broke the news to me gently. "We'd like you to coach," he said. "There's nobody but you." So Red Holzman, the former scout, was the coach of the New York Knickerbockers. No way out now. I really didn't want the job. But how could I hang up Eddie Donovan and Ned Irish? They were in a spot and I always felt I was an organization man. A guy has to have some feeling of responsibility if he has an interest in the people around him.

What about McGuire? They told me we would switch jobs. Dick would do the scouting from now on. That made me feel good. At least it would soften the blow for Dick. He really wasn't being fired by the Knicks. His job was just being changed.

First, we had to go to the Knicks' dressing room and tell the players. They had been asked not to leave. McGuire had to be told. The players suspected something was going on when Donovan scribbled "Practice at 11 A.M. tomorrow" on the blackboard. There had been no practice scheduled.

Donovan asked McGuire to leave the dressing room with him. They came back with Ned Irish and me. They shut the door and Ned took over. "We're now very close to the middle of the season," he told the players. "This will be the start of a new season and, hopefully, a better one. As of 11 A.M. tomorrow, Dick and Red will be swapping jobs."

That was it. I left to join Selma. She had been waiting in my office a long time. I knew she had to be worrying, and when I walked in, her eyes were questioning. "There's a new Knick coach," I announced. "Yeah, who?" she said. "Me," I replied.

When McGuire walked out of the Knicks' dressing room for the last time as coach, his family was waiting in the hall. His wife Terry and their children—Richie, Jr., 8, Leslie, 7 and Mike, 5—had no idea what had just happened.

The kids looked around for pencil and paper. They were like any other youngsters. They wanted autographs from the players. They hung around the dressing room door while Daddy was off on one side telling a reporter the Garden had been fair with him. There were a few words and then some tears.

"What did he say?" inquired Mrs. McGuire. She still didn't know. They soon left the building for the trip back to Huntington. They broke the news to the kids in the car. Only Richie understood and he cried. "Don't cry," said his mother. "Daddy wasn't fired. They just changed his job and that's no disgrace." Richie kept crying.

That is one of the cruelties of sports. There is a human side that people tend to overlook. It is never easy on the guy who is dismissed.

3

The first day on the new job. Some of the players were in the dressing room when I got there for the eleven o'clock practice. A few weren't. I got into my sneakers and shorts and sweat shirt with an eye on my watch—one of those old dollar jobs you used to be able to buy.

Everybody was there but Freddie Crawford, Dick Van Arsdale, Butch Komives, Bill Bradley and Walt Bellamy. Time ran out on them. Crawford was the first to show. "Give Danny five dollars, you're late," I told Freddie. He handed five dollars to Danny Whelan, our trainer. The second one to walk in was Bradley—about four or five minutes late. "Give Danny five dollars," I told him.

Next were Komives and Van Arsdale. They were about ten minutes late. I told them to give Whelan ten dollars each. Butch said he thought the practice was later. "Better check all the time and make sure," I said. Van said they had stopped for breakfast because they figured they were early. "That's the most expensive English muffin and coffee I've ever had," moaned Van Arsdale.

Bellamy was the last to show. He was about fifteen minutes late. It cost him fifteen dollars. He didn't say a word. He paid. I knew the players weren't challenging me. On the first day, that would be silly. But they gave me an opening right away. I didn't have to lecture them on responsibility. I don't believe in lecturing professional ballplayers, anyway. If they don't know what they have to do, they don't belong in the first place. Sometimes you have to remind them of a few things, though.

Ballplaying is hard work. That is, if you really want to be a winner. I was prepared to work hard and I expected the players to do the same thing. Still, I was rather lucky that first day, especially when Bradley was one of those to walk in late. He had the superimage and salary, and the players got a kick out of it when he was fined. They still do whenever I can nail Bill, which is not often.

I had many advantages when I took over. The team was no stranger to me and I was no stranger to the players. I had scouted every one of them when they were in college—even Dick Barnett and Walt Bellamy. They came to the Knicks in trades. Nate Bowman was obtained on waivers. The others were draft picks. They knew me from seeing me at their college games and they knew me from the time I spent around the training camp.

I had been sort of the assistant coach under Fuzzy Levane, Carl Braun, Ed Donovan, Harry Gallatin and Dick McGuire. I would hang around and help out when asked. Naturally, you have your own ideas. It's like the guy in the stands. Everyone is a basketball coach. When I would watch a game, I'd always be thinking of what I would do in each situation.

That is why I had an idea of what I was going to do when I was asked to coach the Knicks. It has nothing to do with changes or who is right or wrong. Some guys like to wear their hair short and others long. To each his own. I only wish I had hair to wear, period. If Dick had been tough on the players, I probably would have been soft. If he had been soft, I probably would have been tough.

I knew this much—the Knicks had good material and the job was to coordinate it and build confidence. They were suffering from growing pains. Cazzie Russell was learning a new position at forward after a rough season in the backcourt as a rookie. Walt Frazier was in his first season and learning. Bill Bradley had played only eleven games.

There was no doubt that the Knicks could score. The problem was to keep the other teams from scoring more. There was only one thing to do—start working hard on defense. That is what I talked about that first day in the dressing room. I told them we would spend most of our time on defense. I told them it was going to be hard work from now on. There would be no days off. Christmas would come in July.

The one message I wanted to get across was that everything the Knicks did was important. It's no different in business. An executive has to establish meaning and enthusiasm and involvement for everyone on his team. There is no other way. It is just as important for Mike Riordan to give a foul at the right time as for Willis Reed to score thirty-five points or grab thirty rebounds.

I never had to explain to Riordan why he was being used mainly to give fouls. He did it because he felt it was important. It was his involvement with the team. He wanted to be a part of the Knicks and he was prepared to do anything to help. He became a solid contributor because he is a fighter and doesn't give up easily.

An attitude like that makes things a lot easier. Riordan would play for any coach like that because that is the way he is. He never felt embarrassed when he was put in with instructions to foul and then was yanked right out. At first, the fans laughed. They thought he was a clown. But they didn't know Mike Riordan, just as a lot of us in the NBA didn't really know Mike Riordan.

I scouted Mike when he was at Providence. He played under a good coach, Joe Mullaney, and had a nice shot from the side as a sophomore. But then Jimmy Walker came along and Mullaney did the only thing a smart coach could do—he built his offense around Walker. That meant Riordan got the ball less and had to concentrate more on defense and rebounding.

Mike wasn't that noticeable with Walker around. When the draft came, we made him a supplementary pick. A supplementary pick is one that takes place after all the teams finish choosing the players they really want. Then they go through the discards. Riordan was one of those. I'm not ashamed to admit it.

A lot of us just didn't have the guts to take him. He was a 6-4 forward who would have to play guard in our league and he just didn't seem to have the shot or credentials. Nobody was going to risk a good pick on him. And when you get past the fourth or fifth pick, you really are filling in. There just aren't that many jobs available on a basketball team. If there were, there wouldn't be enough qualified players in the college draft for any team to wind up with four or five good ones.

Once we were lucky. That was when we wound up with Reed, Barnes, Komives and Bryant. That's the best college draft I can ever remember. We got Bryant on the seventh round. His legs were doubtful. Everyone knew that. You know how he turned out.

There is no such thing as a sleeper in the draft anymore. A Sam Jones can never happen again. Mike Riordan was no sleeper. He was a mistake. Everyone made a mistake on him. We got him and we were lucky. As my wife would say: "It's *beshared*," which means it's written in the cards or something like that.

I had exactly one day of practice before my first game. But there was no sweat. There was absolutely no pressure on me. I didn't ask for the job, so there could not be any heat. Not that it mattered if there was. I would have approached the job the same way. At my age, it was a little difficult to get scared about basketball, anyway.

Naturally, the newspapermen rushed me that first day of practice and wanted to hear some miracles. "Some changes are necessary," I told them. "Certain things will be done differently. We can improve our defense. They have been relaxing too much on defense, and from the outset I'm going to try and get them to think a little more about it."

They wanted more so I gave it to them. "I might start Cazzie instead of Van Arsdale, but starting makes no difference, anyway," I said. They asked about Butch Komives and his obsession about starting. "I'm coming in and not starting any problems," I answered. "I think Komives gives you an honest shake when he's on the court and it depends on what he does and what the team is doing."

I wasn't about to get myself locked in nor did I want anyone to interpret anything I said as a reflection on Mc-Guire. When they asked if I had any special ideas about Bellamy, I said, "I'd like to keep Walter playing as he's been for the last ten games or so." And what about Bradley?

"I'm going to try and play him a lot," I replied. "He's a guy who has talent. He's a guy who can help this club a lot." I meant it. Bradley had a lot of ability. You could see that. He could shoot and handle the ball. He could play defense and he had good basketball instinct. He really never had a chance when he finally decided to play pro ball and the fans knew he was coming to the Knicks.

Nobody, not even Wilt Chamberlain, ever entered the

league with more pressure. Chamberlain had gotten tremendous publicity, but nothing like Bradley. Maybe if Wilt had signed to play in New York instead of Philadelphia he might have gotten more of a reception than Bradley.

Wilt laid out a year after leaving Kansas University following his junior season and played with the Harlem Globetrotters. He still sent tremors throughout the basketball world when he joined the NBA. There had never been a college player who had received as many scholarship offers as Chamberlain. The fans could not wait to see what he could do against Bill Russell in the early stages of his fantastic story with the Celtics.

But Bradley was different. He had the Princeton and Oxford image. He had played some supergames in the Garden and tournaments before becoming a Rhodes Scholar. He was the second coming of Oscar Robertson. He was the savior of the Knicks, finally.

He came to Leone's Restaurant in New York on April 27, 1967, to let the world know he had decided to play pro ball. The Knicks had sweated out the decision ever since they had made Bradley their territorial pick in the 1965 draft. New York and San Francisco had finished with the worst records in their division, so the league permitted each to choose two before the others picked.

That was the last year of the territorial draft, wherein a team could claim a college player anywhere within fifty miles of its franchise. The Knicks took Bradley. The Warriors, allowed the next two, selected Fred Hetzel and a young man named Rick Barry, and the Knicks then chose Dave Stallworth.

"It took the Knicks two years to sign Bill Bradley out of Oxford," wrote columnist Milton Gross of the *New York Post*, "but there was some irritation about him arriving a half hour late for his press conference on the upper floor of Leone's. Somebody suggested he was waiting for the rain to flood Forty-eighth Street so he could walk on the water."

Ned Irish, Ed Donovan and Dick McGuire were there to listen to Bradley, just twenty-three, handle all the questions. "I hope to be of service to other people in my life," he said. "The main thing is to contribute around you, to your neighbors, to your city or whatever. But isn't it presumptuous of a twenty-three-year-old to say what he wants to be, even if I knew, just because I can bounce a ball?"

He was a young man in a spot because he could bounce a ball and he knew it. "I'm asked my opinion on world affairs, economics, disarmament, civil rights," he observed. "I can't understand it." Another time he commented: "I wish I could play basketball against Robertson, West, Havlicek, Baylor, Chamberlain and Russell in a gym, all by ourselves. No spectators, no press, no radio, no television, just play the game. I know it's not practical but I wish it could be that way."

It was hardly that way. Bradley signed a four-year contract for a lot of money and immediately he became Dollar Bill and bugged some people hung up on image. "If he can make a lot of money, it's his privilege, I guess," said one of Bradley's classmates at Ol' Nassau. "I wish I could play that well but it hurts his godlike image. It's like Jerry Lucas, who was a Phi Beta Kappa but is just another good basketball player now. I'm disappointed somewhat."

People who saw in Bradley a political giant of the future, maybe even a President, could not understand how he could stoop to a jock-strap sport. "It might sound trite, but I love the game of basketball," Bill explained for those who did not understand. What was wrong with playing pro sports, anyway? Whizzer White did in football. Of course, he had to settle for a spot on the Supreme Court, so maybe Bradley will pay the price someday.

He was "Mr. President" to his teammates when he reported for active duty on December 7. He had been fulfilling his Air Corps Reserve obligations until then. He stopped by the Garden one day in June for a workout and the sparks flew all around the place. There was a halfcourt scrimmage. Bradley, Frazier and the Van Arsdale twins against Reed, Crawford, Bryant and Riordan.

The first time he got the ball, Bill passed to Dick Van Arsdale for a fifteen footer. Bradley got rid of the ball two more times and then cut off the post to the corner for a jumper that swished through. Everyone was impressed with the workout. Some were overwhelmed.

"He moves real well, with and without the ball," said Coach McGuire. "He isn't afraid to hit the free man and he doesn't miss the open shot. We need someone like that to keep the front line happy."

General manager Donovan next: "Bradley has the strength to play up front if needed," said Eddie. "It might mean giving up something to bigger men but, on the other hand, there is no forward in the league who wouldn't be giving up something to him when he had the ball."

Now the players. Dick Van Arsdale: "I compare him a lot to Oscar. He's that kind of all-around player. He does everything. He's fantastic. You could take away his scoring and he'd still be an asset as a leader. He'll have that effect even on hardened pros because he has everything to be a great player." Willis Reed: "Oh, you can see he'll make it. A man who can move the ball like that and can shoot like that has got to make it. You know how quick that Bryant is and how smart? Now when a man can get the step on Bryant and go around him for the basket, he's good." Em Bryant: "That Bradley will live up to expectations."

That is what Bradley did even before he played his first game in the NBA. It created almost inhuman pressure for him. The pressures off the court also were insufferable. But he is a remarkable young man with a remarkable amount of poise and he handled everything like a real pro.

No rookie in history was asked to do what he did. The Knicks were forced to arrange a press conference in every city on his first swing around the league. That was the kind of excitement he generated. That was the kind of burden he had to carry. That was the kind of demand there was for him.

What's more, he joined the Knicks with the 1967-68 season in progress. He made his first appearance in the twenty-ninth game. He sat in the radio booth and watched his team beat the Baltimore Bullets, 148–117, on December 5. He worked out for the first time two days later. He looked real good. Donovan and McGuire discussed the situation. It was decided that Bradley was ahead of schedule and ready to play.

They picked out the game. It would be against the Detroit Pistons in Madison Square Garden on December 9. The world of pro basketball was going to see Bill Bradley in action.

O

4

"When's Bradley going to play," asked Wilt Chamberlain, the night after Bill had worked out with the Knicks for the first time. He got his answer quickly. One night later in fact.

Bradley walked into the dressing room and found reporters already there and photographers lurking around outside. He appeared calm as he began removing his clothes alongside Butch Komives. Only he knew the turmoil going on inside and he wasn't talking much.

Soon the reporters were asked to leave. The Knick dressing room was closed that early for the first time. Dick McGuire wanted to give Bradley a few minutes to relax. Outside, in the arena, there were over eighteen thousand people waiting for their gladiator to enter.

Ordinarily, the game with the Pistons figured to draw about six thousand, but this was no ordinary night. This was Bill Bradley night and the sellout crowd was waiting to welcome him to pro basketball. "I'd love to have some tickets to the game so I can scalp them," Billy Cunningham of the 76ers had said in anticipation of the certain excitement.

I left the dressing room with Eddie Donovan. I must confess I was anxious to see what was going to happen. Donovan was a lot more nervous. He couldn't stand still. He wandered away and got lost someplace. Then the Knicks came out.

As soon as the fans spotted Number Twenty-four, they went wild. Every move Bradley made was greeted with explosive roars. The old Garden almost disintegrated. Not a sign of emotion, though. Bradley kept shooting and hitting and adding to the level of hysteria. "I didn't try to delineate what it meant," he was to say after the game. (He meant he didn't try to figure it out.)

John Condon, the Garden public address announcer and the best of them all, got carried away, apparently. He was supposed to save Bradley for last in his introductions. He was supposed to say: "And now the newest member of the Knicks—Number Twenty-four, Bill Bradley," but he forgot and announced the singing of the national anthem.

Condon amended things by introducing Bradley after the "Star Spangled Banner." Wow! You almost forgot there was going to be a ball game. You got the feeling everyone was there just to see Bradley in a Knick uniform and then was going to leave after he was introduced.

The game did start and Bradley got into it. Not at the start. That would be too much to ask. McGuire couldn't do that to him. Dick didn't even bring Bill in as his first sub in the backcourt. Komives got the assignment. He also got booed by the fans. They expected Bradley.

They got him at the start of the second period. The Knicks were leading, 35–23, when Bradley got off the bench. Cheers. He joined the huddle during the time-out. Cheers. He checked in at the scorer's table. Cheers. He trotted onto the floor. Cheers.

Leonard Koppett, the historian of *The New York Times* recorded the sports event this way: "It was 9:04 P.M., December 9, 1967—exactly two years and seven months (and approximately ten hours) from the time the Knicks had drafted him, knowing he was a Rhodes Scholar who would be going to Oxford first."

Seven minutes later, Detroit was in front, 49–46, and Bryant came in for Bradley. The crowd gave Bill a polite round of applause. Bradley played twenty minutes, hit three of his six shots, grabbed five rebounds and had two assists.

It was not a sensational beginning. He made many mistakes. What's more, the Detroit Pistons won. But *The New York Times* still was carried away by the hysteria of Bradley's first game in a Knick uniform. "Pistons Top Knicks, 124–121, Despite Bradley's 8 Points," was the banner an overwrought deskman put on the story.

Back in the dressing room. "Too much pressure," observed coach McGuire. "I know he's getting big money but the pressure on him is terrific." Bradley was sitting on a bench against a wall. He was nowhere in sight, obliterated by a mob of reporters, photographers and radio men, who were fighting to jam their mikes down Bradley's throat. "Unbelievable," said Cazzie Russell, who had created his own excitement the season before as a rookie —but nothing like this. "I expect the CIA in here any minute to rescue the President."

Willis Reed, the captain, looked on from the other side of the room. "I kidded Cazzie when he went through this last year, but you can't neglect the public," said Willis. Had it ever happened to him? "No one knew me when I came here and no one knows me now," answered Reed, his white teeth flashing in a patent smile.

"There might be pressure if I didn't improve in ten or twenty games," said Bradley as he handled the full court press by the news media. "It's just noise," was his reaction to the tumult he had created. He then moved to a room that had been set up strictly for the television people. Someone suggested that any minute a band would break out with 'Hail to the Chief.'

Bradley managed to survive it all. He faced more excitement in one night than I did in my entire career. I never encountered such pressure even when I was a kid playing handball at P.S. 178 in Brooklyn for a quarter a game.

It was remarkable. He had been on duty at McGuire Air Force Base, New Jersey, and did not arrive until two hours before the game. Afterward he traveled to Princeton, where he was staying, and arrived at around three in the morning. Two hours later he was on his way back to McGuire. "It's not a one-game challenge," he said. "The enthusiasm was great and I was sorry I couldn't respond with skill."

The Knicks were happy to have him. They promised that Bradley would be there a long time. "It takes most rookies months to adjust," said Komives, for example, "but it'll take him weeks." Komives had gotten to know Bradley quicker than anyone. Butch made Bill his personal project.

"I figured someone had to make him feel relaxed and comfortable," explained Komives. So Butch took it upon himself to help Bradley round out his square image. Komives kidded Bill about his clothes and girls constantly. It was Butch's way of contributing to the team by helping Bradley.

One day, shortly after Bradley joined the Knicks, he made the mistake of telling Komives he was going out to buy a suit. "I hope it isn't going to be blue with a red 'S' on it," Butch told Superman. Another time, Bill revealed he had just bought two suits and the trousers had cuffs. "You got cuffs so you can catch all your money when it drops," suggested Komives.

Bradley would laugh. So would all the Knicks. He managed to ease right into the team despite the outside pressure. All the players liked to tease him and he had the temperament to accept and enjoy it. "When you're president," Dick Barnett said to him, "I wanna be secretary of the treasury."

It was a "ball" to Bradley. He turned pro because he loved basketball, but he really never figured it could be this much fun. He had his problems on the court for a long time. And then there were those time-consuming press conferences in every city. They even scheduled an extra one for him in Evansville, Indiana, where the Chicago Bulls were promoting a game with the Knicks. "I'm beginning to wonder how many more cities we are going into," he smiled.

Very few people know it, but Bradley has an impish sense of humor. One day in San Francisco, some of the Knicks decided to go shopping. Van Arsdale and Komives took Bradley to a department store. They bought some stuff and went back to the Jack Tar Hotel.

A few hours later, Danny Whelan was down in the lobby. He was waiting for the players. Whelan is always the first one down. He is the Knicks' den mother. He makes sure the bus is there, handles the players' aches and gripes, collects the fines, tells stories and makes the players laugh.

Danny Whelan, in fact, is a gem. He was the guy who invented the Green Weenie symbol for the 1960 Pittsburgh Pirates. You may recall they won the pennant and beat the Yankees in the World Series. I can see why. With Danny around, it is almost impossible not to be winner. He is a funny guy and a top trainer. The players feel very comfortable around him. I am not ashamed to admit that he was greatly responsible for the excellent rapport among the Knicks.

I don't know what I would have done without him. He is chancellor of the exchequer and makes the collection of fines so pleasant, the players do not fight too hard about paying. And you should know how tough it is to get five or ten dollars out of some guys.

By the end of a season, I've generally gotten them all for something. Sometimes it might even be for coming onto the court with a shoelace untied. The money goes towards a party at the end of the season, yet there will be growls and gripes when it comes time to pay.

Dave Stallworth always is the toughest to nail. He is always on time. He never gives me a chance to fine him for anything. The fines are really nothing. They are mostly for showing up late and keeping others waiting. Everyone gets an itinerary. If we are at home, the players are given their entire schedule for the week. If we are on the road, they have an itemized program for the entire trip.

There are no excuses. It is all there and if a player does not show on time, then it is his responsibility. Stallworth was impossible. Whelan and I cooked up all kinds of schemes to get him. No good. I finally made it near the end of the 1969-70 season—just before we went into the playoffs and won the championship.

We were flying home from Boston. I was talking to Whelan and not even thinking about Stallworth, when suddenly I looked over at him. I jumped out of my seat. "Rave," I said. "I've finally got you." The Rave was aware of what I meant. He was part of the little game we were playing. "No way, Red," he said. "I've done nothing."

I gave him one of my better leers. "Yes, you have," I said, rubbing my hands together like old man Scrooge. "You're drinking beer on the plane and you're not supposed to do that." I had no such rule but I sounded so convincing, Stalls gave Dan Whelan five dollars. I made sure Danny returned the money to him after the season.

Anyway, Whelan was standing in the lobby of the Jack Tar Hotel in San Francisco, waiting for all the players to come down. He was watching the elevators. The door of one opened and Danny looked once and then twice. "I saw this freak coming out, and I couldn't believe it," he said.

Out of the elevator stepped a guy with long hippie hair, a chain and medallion around his neck and wearing dark glasses. "This guy walks right up to me and past me and I still don't recognize him until he walks away," explained Whelan. "Then I see that crazy walk and I know who it is."

Yes, it was Bill Bradley. He wore the same disguise when he left the Knicks' dressing room after the game that night. There wasn't a photographer around. They missed the picture of the year.

That was funny. I'll tell you a Bradley incident that was not so funny. Oh, how I remember it! I had just finished my first day on the job as coach of the Knicks. It had been a rather busy one. First, the players walking in late and being fined. Then, practice and the start of a new team defense I hoped would tie up the loose ends and make something of the Knicks.

From the very beginning, I would say I spent about 80 percent of the time on defense. I never changed it. We spend only 20 per cent of the time on offense. We never work more than an hour and a half. I think that is plenty. I know just what I want to do and we do it. There isn't a wasted minute.

I started out by telling the players we were going to use a three-quarter press from now on. We were going to pick up the other team deep and make the ball handlers work a little harder to bring the ball down. We worked on position. I was surprised how quickly they grasped it.

Walt Frazier, Phil Jackson, Dick Barnett, Willis Reed and the others fit right into it. We put in a hard day's work and I liked the way the players reacted. They were very receptive. They all listened. There were no conversations between the players watching the drills. There was no one wandering off at one end to shoot some baskets while we discussed fundamentals at the other.

It was a crash program because we were playing the next night. Los Angeles was coming into the Garden. That meant Jerry West and Elgin Baylor, who have given many a coach sleepless nights. I went to bed early. I usually do when I am home. I sleep well no matter what.

I don't know exactly the time, but I think the phone rang around eleven o'clock. It was Eddie Donovan. Some friend. Here I'm on the job only one day and already he is calling me at home and breaking up my sleep. "Yeah, Eddie," was my greeting. "Red," he said. "You won't believe this but Bradley's been hit by a car. It's not serious but I thought I'd better let you know right away."

Bradley hit by a car? How? It was simple. At least, it was simple the way Bradley explained it. "I slept late and went out about ten o'clock at night to get something to eat," the story began. "I was walking across Eighth Avenue and Fifty-fifth Street when I suddenly saw this car coming at me."

The car came along and Bradley stepped off the curb. Fortunately for Bill, the car, an MG driven by a young lady wasn't going too fast.

Bradley spotted the MG or the girl out of the corner of his eye. He tried to jump out of the way, but was struck a glancing blow in the right hip. He hit the ground, hurt his right wrist and suffered a small cut on his left ankle.

"I must've twisted around or something," he said, trying to explain the assortment of injuries. "He was lucky it was raining," suggested Dr. Kazuo Yanagisawa, the team doctor. "His hand slid when he tried to break his fall. It might have been serious otherwise."

The night of my first game, Bradley was in taking whirlpool while the players were getting ready to face the

Lakers. When the game started, he sat next to me on the bench in his street clothes. I wish I could say everything worked out fine that night. We lost.

It was no real tragedy. Los Angeles won, 126–115. West shot 13-for-27 (thirty points) and Baylor 12-for-26 (twenty-nine points). You would not say it was one of those debuts they call auspicious. But I saw some good things out there. So did West. "Their bench looked real good," said Jerry. "Especially Phil Jackson."

Jackson, a rookie at the time, played twenty-two minutes because Reed and Bellamy got into foul trouble. Phil hit 7-for-11, grabbed nineteen rebounds and blocked several shots. What impressed me was the way Jackson handled himself in our semipress. The whole team defense looked good in spite of only one practice session.

Before the game I had told the players to go all out on defense. They shouldn't worry about getting tired. It was important to get them off right. So I used thirteen substitutions in the first nineteen minutes. I used the shaking-'em-up system. We got in front by two points after trailing from the start but could not hold on. "We were too darned tired to do anything after we took the lead," said Van Arsdale. "Now we can start all over again."

That was nice to hear. The enthusiasm was there. The talent was there. All we had to do was to keep working hard on our defense. It was December 29 and I laid out the practice schedule for the team. There would be a meeting the next day and practice Sunday and Monday.

Someone mentioned that Monday was New Year's. I had to remind them that Christmas and New Year's would be in the summer for them. We had a game coming up with Oscar Robertson and Cincinnati in Philadelphia on Tuesday and we had lost five straight now. I was 0-for-1 myself and I didn't want to go too long before I got in the win column.

Dick McGuire, the lucky guy, was in Los Angeles scouting. There, but for the grace of a bad start by the Knicks, go I. Oh, well. I had problems of my own now. Dick was far away from all the aggravation. I was the one who had to figure out how to get more out of Reed and Bellamy when they were playing together. I had to fit Frazier and Jackson, our rookies, into the right place where their talents would be properly employed. I had to keep Bradley company on the bench while he recuperated from his attack by the MG. I had to do something about Cazzie Russell.

5

There was a strong relationship between the careers of Bradley and Russell. They met for the first time in college when Cazzie's top-ranked Michigan team played Bradley's Princeton team in the 1964 Holiday Festival. They both were drafted by the Knicks and signed multiple-year package deals.

Futhermore, they each started in the backcourt as pros because they were considered in-between sizes—too small to play forward. They both switched up front, eventually. Bradley got his big chance when Cazzie broke an ankle. To top it all, it was Russell's team blazer that Dollar Bill wore the day the Knicks announced he had signed a contract.

The fans in New York never will forget that Holiday Festival semi-final between Princeton and Michigan. It was won by the Wolverines when Bradley fouled out and Cazzie broke out. "I have never seen one player so humiliate one team, a top-ranked team," observed Joe Lapchick after Bradley had scored forty-one points and was voted Most Valuable Player 22-1.

One vote was cast for Russell. He has had many more

popularity votes since from the New York and NBA fans who have watched his sensational shooting. There is no one in the league who can break a game open faster. When Cazzie gets hot, forget it. He is an exciting player and a demanding one. No one works harder. No one takes care of himself better.

Cazzie is the guy who introduced health foods to the Knicks. He leads the league in wheat germ and carrot juice. Dick Barnett refers to him as The Wheat Germ Kid. Tricky Dick should know. Cazzie has him eating the stuff. Me? Give me steak or scungilli and you can have the wheat fields of the world.

The Knicks got Russell in a toss of the coin with the Detroit Pistons. General manager Ed Coil called and lost, and Cazzie belonged to New York. It really hurt the Pistons at the time. They needed Russell badly. He had the Michigan image and would have sold tickets. But the Pistons had to settle for Dave Bing—which is almost like the Bob Cousy story. Not quite, but almost.

You remember that one. The Chicago Stags, one of the original members of the Basketball Association of America that was to become the NBA, had to give up after four seasons. No more money. Commissioner Maurice Podoloff, on the advice of the board of governors, announced that the top three players would go to New York, Philadelphia and Boston.

Max Zaslofsky, one of the best scorers in the league, was considered the catch. Then there was Andy Phillip, one of the Illinois Whiz Kids. And finally a rookie named Bob Cousy from Holy Cross.

Boston could have had Cousy as a territorial choice but passed him up to take Chuck Cooper, a great college forward from Duquesne and the first Negro drafted into the NBA. Now comes one of those strange bounces I keep talking about. The three names were dropped in a hat.

Ned Irish picked first and came up with Zaslofsky and was happy. Eddie Gottlieb was next and he pulled out Phillip and was happy. The Celtics were stuck with Cousy. Any questions?

Want another coincidence? The owner of the Stags was a man named Arthur Morse. He was a Chicago attorney who had gotten into basketball through his affiliation with DePaul University at a time when George Mikan was playing there. Morse went on to promote college doubleheaders in Chicago Stadium that featured DePaul and Big Ten teams. He was the Ned Irish of the midwest, if you please.

It was the natural step to invite Morse to take over a franchise when the Basketball Association of America was formed in 1946 by people who controlled buildings. They were fundamentally hockey operators looking for another sport to fill dates. Pro basketball was it. Morse got the Chicago area because he already was promoting college basketball in Chicago Stadium.

Now let's take a trip in the time machine. It is twenty years later—1966. A young basketball sensation named Cazzie Russell has finished four years at Michigan and is considered the prize of the college draft. He becomes the property of the Knicks. He needs a lawyer. He gets one. The attorney's name is Arthur Morse. Yes, that Arthur Morse.

Morse came to Russell with credentials. Arthur had negotiated a few pro football deals. This was at the time of the Joe Namath breakthrough with Sonny Werblin and the Jets. The Chicago lawyer went to the Knicks with fundamentally the same concept for Cazzie. He talked tax dollars. Morse had prepared a complete program. The Garden accepted.

Russell can tell his grandchildren he was the first rookie in the NBA to receive anything like the package he received. Needless to say, Cazzie entered pro basketball with a lot of pressure. It was decided to play him in the backcourt. He was asked to play Oscar Robertson, Jerry West, Hal Greer, Lennie Wilkens and Dave Bing.

It was a matter of circumstances. The Knicks had plenty of forwards—Reed, Van Arsdale, Stallworth, Neil Johnson and Henry Akin. They had only one big shooting guard—Dick Barnett. The others were Komives, Bryant, Crawford and Dave Deutsch. So, out of necessity, and because 6-5 in those days was considered kind of small for a forward, Cazzie was asked to play backcourt.

He really was out of position. But he never complained. He did what was asked of him though he probably would have preferred to play up front. He tried his best to handle the superior speed of the other backcourt men. He was able to make them pay with his shooting.

The Knicks thought Cazzie would improve with experience and be able to make the quicker guards pay even more. When the situation changed, Cazzie went to forward and then I came along and figured he would be most valuable coming off the bench for us. Cazzie, no doubt, could start on any other team. But on the Knicks, he was asked to do what would help the team the most. He did it without questioning why. There are only a few in the league who can come off the bench like Cazzie and destroy the other team. I can only think of two other players who were capable of doing it—John Havlicek and Frank Ramsey.

The most difficult thing for any coach to sell ballplayers is that starting doesn't mean a thing. Some insist they cannot play their game if they don't start. Komives was like that.

Butch was one fine competitor. He'd put his head through the wall for you. But for some strange reason, he had this thing about starting. He could handle the booing in the Garden to a point but, if he wasn't in the opening lineup, it bugged him. He worked himself up to the stage where he got mad at McGuire and asked to be traded.

You must understand that Dick had been Komives's top defender. Butch, without a doubt, was the most abused player the Knicks ever had and for no good reason. He came to the team as a shooter. I should know because I scouted him. He was a great scorer at Bowling Green. He was more noticeable at the time than a teammate named Nate Thurmond.

Komives, like Cazzie in his rookie year, was a victim of circumstances. Butch was a shooter but was asked to make the play. He was a good ball handler but not a natural. Ball handlers are born, not made.

Ball handlers also have the ball a lot and the fans are always looking at the ball. So if a good pass is not made, the passer cannot hide. Komives paid the penalty of being a manufactured passer. He was booed as though he was the enemy. "Butch is a hard-nosed player," McGuire would say in his defense. "He is doing all that is being asked. He gives 100 per cent all the time. What more do they want from him?"

It did not help. They still booed Butch every time he threw the ball away. He tolerated it as best he could when he was starting and playing. But that stopped when winning stopped (or really never started) at the beginning of the 1967-68 season.

The Knicks began the 1967-68 season with high hopes but without Frazier. He was on the injured list for five games when they opened in the Garden against San Francisco and won, 124–122, on two clutch shots by Cazzie. He hit the first with sixteen seconds to go to put the team ahead, 122–120, and the winner from the corner with one second left.

San Francisco was playing without Rick Barry. He had

jumped to the American Basketball Association. But the Knicks felt good about winning the first one. They were to wait awhile before they won again. Five straight defeats carried them to Oakland and the first serious signs of distress.

McGuire called a gripe session in the motel. He stocked the room with beer and sandwiches. He was right. It was a long siege. The coach and players talked it out for two hours. "We have instituted a series of fines," reported Reed, the captain. "We're charging three dollars for being late for practice and there will be fines for being late for buses and things like that. We feel it is better to discipline ourselves." (Even fines were cheaper in those days.)

McGuire did not sit still. He decided to start Reed, instead of Bellamy, at center, and open with Johnson at forward. "I'm not benching Bells," Dick explained. "I've just got to try something different." It didn't help that night. San Francisco won, and the Knicks had lost six in a row.

Reed took care of that almost by himself the next night in Los Angeles. Willis pumped fifty-three points, and the Knicks won, 129–113. McGuire started Jackson up front and Reed at center. He used Cazzie and Van Arsdale together at forward in the third period when the game was put away. "It feels good to win one," sighed McGuire.

But Dick, usually a very calm guy, was aggravating himself sick over the situation. The frustration was getting to him. Eddie Donovan had flown out to the Coast to get some first-hand information as to what was going on. "I told him he was a damned fool," recalled Eddie. "I told him to take it out on the players or give the damned thing up. I told him not to kill himself—he was too nice a guy."

McGuire tried. The Knicks won a few, lost a few. A coach in that predicament cannot sit still. He makes changes. He plays the hot hand if there is a hot hand.

Bryant got one along the way and McGuire did the only thing he could do under the conditions—he began playing Emmette ahead of Komives.

Frazier also was back by then. And there was Barnett. So there really was not much time left for Butch. The Knicks had improved to 8-7 when they went to Boston for a game with San Diego, then an expansion club. Komives and McGuire had it out. The Knicks lost, but Butch did not play at all that night. "No reason at all, I just didn't get him into it," was McGuire's explanation.

It was obvious that Dick was following Donovan's advice. The coach was not going to worry himself sick over the players. He was going to do what he felt he had to do and that was it. About a week and one game later it happened. Komives blasted off. He was sick and tired of being booed in New York. And he was annoyed because he wasn't playing.

"I have nothing against the organization," said Butch. "Nothing against Madison Square Garden. I'm twenty-six. I've got a lot of good years in me. I've proved I can play in this league. The people would never let me play in New York, though."

He said he tolerated the abuse as long as he was playing. He suggested that his coach had finally succumbed to the fans and benched him. "I used to get upset when Harry [Gallatin] pulled me out of the game and the fans booed, but under McGuire, he never took me out when I made a mistake," Komives continued. "That is what built up my confidence. I feel they [the fans] are the reason for me not playing all the time."

It was an agonizing moment for McGuire. All coaches go through moments like that at one time or another. There always are some players who feel they should get more playing time. Komives felt he had earned greater consideration for doing the job as best he could.

McGuire, like any other coach, sympathized with Butch and had played him a lot, but the team was losing. Something had to be done. It's a funny thing about sports. Generally speaking, the players are there long after a coach is gone. There are two sides to the coin but there is only one object—*win*. Only the coach can decide how to do that.

"The thing that disturbs me the most," Komives kept insisting, "is that I changed my game to play with Barnett and Bellamy. I went from a shooter to making the play because they said there was no one else on the team. Last year, the people were saying what the team needed was assists. I even prepared myself mentally to come off the bench."

The game has changed in that respect since I played it. When I was at Rochester, starting meant more than it does today. It was a different game. The twenty-four-second clock changed that. Today's game is so fast, you must go to your bench more. It is really impossible for players to go forty-eight minutes, unless you're a Chamberlain, Bill Russell, Nate Thurmond or Lew Alcindor. Even then, I question the wisdom of it.

Komives didn't like what was happening to him and, from his viewpoint, he was entitled to better consideration. That didn't make him right because he felt that way. Donovan and McGuire, two good basketball men, felt otherwise. The general manager called Butch to his office and told him so. "If I was thirty-one or thirty-two," Komives had said, "I wouldn't say too much. But with Bradley coming soon, the scene looks dull. I don't want to be buried young. If they don't want me, why don't they get rid of me?"

Donovan, who had invested a lot of time and patience and blood, trying to build a winner for the Garden, had a few answers. "The coach never takes anyone out of the ball game," he reminded his upset player. "The player takes himself out." He also told Butch he had a certain responsibility to the team and his teammates and that his contract did not guarantee he start or even how many minutes he should play.

"You know, Butch," Donovan then pointed out. "There's nothing to stop us from sending you to Allentown and paying your salary there." I felt sorry for Butch. So did Donovan and McGuire. They really liked him. They appreciated how hard he always played. All they were trying to do was get Butch to recognize that understanding is not a one-way street. A player has a tendency to think only as a player or about himself. A coach has to think of everyone.

Yes, it was tough on Komives—just as it is tough on guys who play less. But it was tougher on McGuire. He had to contend with twelve different personalities. They all wanted to play. Dick also was getting paid to see that those twelve players won or else, so he had to make his own decisions—right or wrong.

I'll say this about Butch: once he cooled off, it was as though nothing ever happened. He put out whenever McGuire called on him.

Now, Cazzie approached his situation differently. He had feelings, just like Komives. I'm sure he would have preferred to start for the Knicks all the time and bled a little when I eventually concluded that his maximum contribution in our situation was coming off the bench. But he never said a word to me when I made the change, and I never said a word to him. Once, maybe, come to think of it.

It was late in the season on our last swing through the West before we won the championship. First place was a lock and the team was moving along easily towards the playoffs. Then, one day, a reporter brought up the Bradley and Russell situation in his paper. He questioned the intelligence of starting Bill over Cazzie. He raked over some hot coals.

I couldn't blame the newspaperman. He was looking for a story and he was rather new on the assignment, so he was not familiar with the background. But he wrote a few things that seemed to upset Cazzie. I had a meeting with Caz and straightened it out. I think.

McGuire had Cazzie at forward when Bradley appeared for his first game. It was a loser. Bradley's second game was even more frustrating. The pressure was building on Bill and McGuire, but not necessarily in that order. "I don't envy Dick," said Richie Guerin as he brought the St. Louis Hawks into the Garden for the first time that season. The Hawks were leading the Western Division with twenty-two and seven, while the Knicks were fourth in the East with twelve and seventeen.

Guerin was aware of the pressure on McGuire to win. Everyone kept talking about the material. There were a lot of names on the Knicks and a lot of big college reputations, but there is more to team basketball than that. Every team in the league has players who were great in college. A lot of things must happen for a team to become a winner. And don't forget, there can be only one winner each season.

"As long as Dick has Bradley in uniform, he has to play him," Guerin pointed out. "And if he plays him, Dick can be jeopardizing a victory because Bradley can't be ready. If he doesn't play him, I can hear them booing Dick now."

Guerin was not questioning Bradley's ability to play in the league. "He might even kill us," Rich said. "But he's been away two years. Bradley has to prove himself. Not that I doubt that he can, but to me he is Bill Bradley, collegian, right now. I know Bradley has a lot of poise and all those things but he's just a kid."

McGuire decided to start Bradley against the Hawks.

It might ease the pressure. Coming off the bench was asking too much. Guerin showed no sympathy. He put Joe Caldwell on Bradley and you know what that means. You know how Joe dogs his man. You know how he can pressure a ball handler.

Bradley did very well under the circumstances. Caldwell played him for forty-seven minutes, which can feel like a lifetime. Bradley managed to hit 10-for-16 (twenty-three points). He got five rebounds and seven assists. Not bad at all for a rookie under tremendous pressure in his second game. One thing was wrong—the Knicks lost in double overtime.

It was a tough one; the kind that was becoming all too familiar for McGuire. The Knicks actually led by seventeen points with six and a half minutes to go but still did not win. Guerin ordered the full-court press that usually bothered the Knicks, and the Hawks tied the score on a basket by Lennie Wilkens with ten seconds to go in regulation.

The way it was tied really hurt. Wilkens had just missed with twenty-four seconds to go and the Knicks leading by two. Walt Bellamy cleared the rebound and the ball finally wound up with Bradley in front court. All Bill had to do was kill the clock, but he was carried away by the flow of the game.

He shot. Bill Bridges smothered the ball. Wilkens tied it and the Hawks went on to win it. I had watched the game from the mezzanine press box and could hardly believe it. But I could understand. Bradley had not been through anything like this before and he made the kind of mistake that a veteran is likely to make sometimes.

Bradley didn't have much to say after the game. "I don't enjoy any game I lose," he volunteered.

I felt sorry mostly for McGuire. I knew how much every victory meant to him. To lose like this, after being in front by seventeen so late in the game, was murder. But Bradley had looked really good. Maybe he would come around fast after all and save things.

"He played extremely well for a rookie," said Caldwell, who had been Bradley's Olympic teammate in 1964. "I was trying to get his attention. You try anything on a rookie. I was told to keep him from getting the ball. You can't psych him, he's a real pro. I couldn't completely stop him."

The defeat did nothing to help McGuire or the Knicks. But I was impressed by the way the Hawks used the full-court press. It was a dangerous weapon in their hands. Zelmo Beaty, Paul Silas, Caldwell, Wilkens and Bridges did all the work. Wilkens played the least at forty-five minutes. Five men did the job. I stored that away in my mind.

6

It was late in the preseason game with the Chicago Bulls in Herricks, Long Island. The Knicks won, 117–107, but rookie Walt Frazier twisted an ankle in the closing seconds. "Frazier stretched the inside ligament of his right ankle," we announced the next day, "and will be out for a week to ten days."

A tough blow. Frazier, the Knicks' top draft choice, had looked so great in camp and now, in only his second exhibition game, he was lost with an injury. "He was the best player in the draft," coach Dick McGuire had said when the Knicks took Frazier. That was the year Earl Monroe and Jimmy Walker came out.

Walker, the Providence star, went to Detroit as the Number One choice of the 1967 draft. Jimmy signed a good contract for four years. Bill Bradley already had announced his intention of playing for the Knicks and not the ABA.

Commissioner Walter Kennedy did not overlook this latest boost for the NBA in its competition with the new league. "Bradley and Walker were the two most important players available," the commissioner proclaimed. "Signing both speaks for itself." Mr. Kennedy and a lot of people changed their minds a little after Frazier came into the league.

We had Frazier as our Number One choice all the way in that draft. We were interested in no one else. We had a lot of nervous moments. We were set to pick fifth. Detroit was first, then Baltimore, Chicago and Detroit, again.

The Pistons were getting Los Angeles's first pick from the LaRusso deal. When Rudy refused to report, Commissioner Kennedy ordered the Lakers to substitute their top draft choice for Detroit. So the Pistons were slated to get the fourth player and the Knicks the fifth.

Detroit made no secret that Walker was going to be Number One and surprised nobody. Now the worrying began at our table. We had heard that the Baltimore Bullets were interested in Earl (The Pearl) Monroe, but you can never be sure of those things until they happen. We weren't even sure we could sign Frazier if we were lucky enough to get him.

We had seen him play many times and under the right conditions. We liked the way he reacted to pressure in the National Invitation Tournament. In the first half, he was the ball handler and concentrated on running the team. Then, in the second half, when it looked as though Marquette was going to beat Southern Illinois, he took charge of everything. He passed, he played defense, he stole the ball and he did the scoring.

The Salukis came from behind to win. Frazier was voted the Most Valuable Player easily and we were impressed. So were the other scouts. The place was loaded with them. They had to see what we saw. Walt had been just too outstanding to remain a secret.

But we went ahead as though only we knew about him. There is no other way if you are interested in a player. A scout has to evaluate everyone and everything as though

54

every player is available. I was the scout and I had created my own filing system. Everybody has his own way.

You should check out everything about a player. His personality, his ambition, his school record, his playing background, his physical equipment, his playing style and habits, his IQ. Yes, an IQ can tell you something in some cases. I know one ballplayer who had a very low IQ and was drafted very high. He never really made it big.

I came up with a work sheet after many years of trial and error. I broke everything down into categories. Anything that would give a comprehensive picture of a player. That made it a lot easier when I sat with Eddie Donovan and prepared our list for the draft.

I have three pages on the questionnaire I compiled for my own benefit. There are five categories: *Scholastic, Background, Physical, Basketball, General.* There are subdivisions for each. Under Scholastic, for example, there are such things as: Will he get a degree? Will he go to grad school? Was he ever redshirted? Ineligible? Transfer? Junior college transfer? Missed year due to illness or injury? What illness? What injury?

Under Basketball, I had every possible question I could think of. Here's just one. Defense: Tries all the time? Fights over screens? Does he overplay? Head turner? Nobody can score on him? Picks up high? Bad defensive habits? Can't spell it?

Under General, there were other sports. Football? Baseball? Honors won? Is he pro caliber? Does he rate bonus? Large bonus? *Family:* Poor? Average? Wealthy? Split home? Parents dead? *Pro Ball:* Not sure? Wants it bad? Other offers? They are? *Will he:* Pay price? Go through wall if asked? Hit floor for loose ball? Accept responsibility? Wants ball in clutch? Chokes in clutch? Is he cocky? Fears no one? Fancy to a fault? Poor basketball sense?

Will he take last shot? Does he dominate game as he should?

I even came up with an 'If' section in the Physical category. *If:* He lost twenty pounds? Gained twenty pounds? Had three more inches? Could jump? Could shoot? Was faster?

There were many more. Too many to itemize. Anyway, a guy's entitled to keep a little of his own secrets, isn't he?

My work sheet told us a lot about Frazier. One thing it revealed was that he had been redshirted. He sat out a season of eligibility after a fine sophomore year at Southern Illinois. A physical education major, he had missed enough classes and examinations to flunk.

"I was depressed," Walt explained. "I didn't know if I wanted to study. I was doubting I could stay there. I didn't think that all I had to do to stay was study. I came to terms with myself in the summer. I wore weights on my legs while I worked in a cotton factory. When I went back to school, I took the hardest courses I could take. And I worked out three and one-half hours a day, on isometrics and weights, and scrimmaging."

He went back to school and led his team to the NIT championship in 1967. He also found himself eligible for the NBA draft as a junior. The rule is, a player becomes eligible when his class has been graduated. Frazier, technically, was a member of the class being graduated in 1967, though he had another year of college eligibility if he wanted it.

Vince Boryla came to the Knicks the same way. Vinny started at Notre Dame, went into service and then entered the University of Denver. He played one season at Denver but his class at Notre Dame had been graduated. Ned Irish made a deal with him and became the first owner in the NBA to take advantage of the rule. Vinny gave up his last year of college eligibility to play for the Knicks.

The author rises to the occasion.

Commissioner Walter Kennedy honors Coach of the Year.

You can't win 'em all.

DICK BARNETT (12)

Tricky Dick makes Jerry West a spectator.

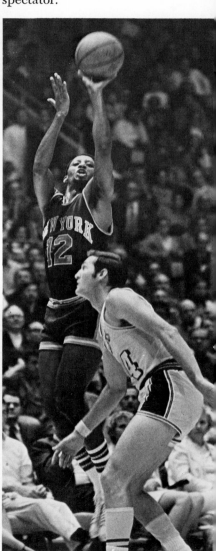

Dave Stallworth runs interference.

BILL BRADLEY (24)

Above right: In a painful moment. *Below:* Trying to shake Jack Marin.

DAVE DeBUSSCHERE (22)

Above right: Trying to make a
point with Billy Cunningham.

Making a point with Bill Bridges.

WALT FRAZIER (10)

Pistol Pete Maravich is going his way.

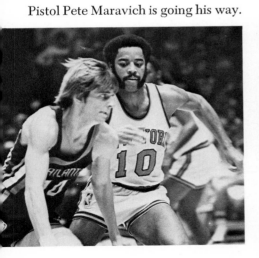

Right: Now where did he go?

WILLIS REED (19)

Up and over Wilt Chamberlain.

Battles Lew Alcindor.

CAZZIE RUSSELL (33)

Breaks an ankle.

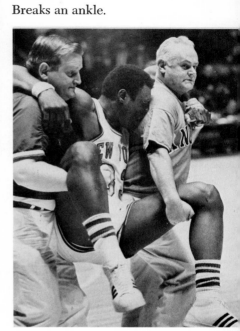

Below: Back in action.

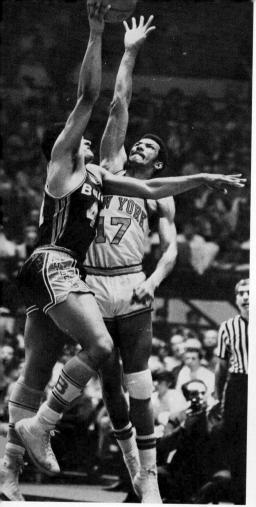

Nate Bowman doing his thing.

Bill Hosket gets things going.

Phil Jackson caught in traffic.

Don May, one of the Dayton boys.

Mike Riordan, determined as ever.

Dave Stallworth picks on an easy one — Oscar Robertson.

Left: John Warren, a rookie on the move. *Right:* Earl Monroe vs Frazier. Speed and more speed.

A little something extra from Willis Reed.

The Mod World.

Eddie Donovan

Co-author Leonard Lewin interviews
Willis Reed.

Dick McGuire

Trainer Danny Whelan,
The Den Mother.

The Knicks' secret weapon.

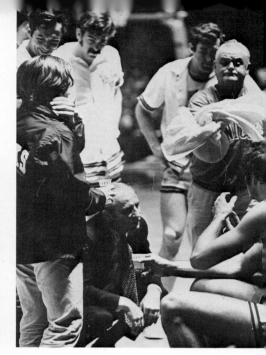

The author with Chairman
Irving Mitchell Felt, right, and
President Edward S. Irish, left.

"'Hey, sit down. It's not over yet.' I was screaming at the players."

"We're Number One."

Victors Bill Bradley, Nate Bowman and Dave DeBusschere (with Howard Cosell) are photographed by George Kalinsky.

Victory champagne.

We knew Frazier was in the same position. We did a little investigating and learned he was interested in playing pro ball if he got the right deal. We were prepared to go high if we could get him. We heard stories that the Chicago Bulls had their eyes on him. No surprise, since he was playing practically in their backyard.

The 1967 draft started and Walker went. Up stepped Baltimore. "Baltimore takes Earl Monroe, 6-3, of Winston-Salem," it was announced. Two more to go. Now Chicago. We looked over at the Bulls' table. "Chicago takes Clem Haskins, 6-3, of Western Kentucky," was the announcement.

One more. Just one more. "Maybe," I said to Ed Donovan and Ned Irish at our table. Detroit was picking again. We were saying to ourselves: "The Pistons don't need another backcourt man. They have Bing and Walker and Eddie Miles and Tom Van Arsdale. What would they do with Frazier?" It was wishful thinking.

"Detroit," the announcement finally came, "picks Sonny Dove, 6-8, of St. John's." We were in. But we didn't want to look too anxious. We played it cool. When Commissioner Kennedy announced: "New York," meaning we were up, we took our time. We went into a huddle.

Donovan nodded as though we had finally made up our minds. "New York takes Walt Frazier, 6-3, of Southern Illinois," was our announcement. It was amazing. We had gotten the man we wanted, again. In 1964 it was Barnes and Reed, the next year Bradley and Dick Van Arsdale, then Cazzie Russell and now Frazier.

That was quite a run. There were others. There was Dave Stallworth in 1965, along with Bradley and Van Arsdale, and Phil Jackson in 1967 after we chose Frazier.

"We figured it would be Walker to Detroit, Monroe to Baltimore, either Frazier or Haskins to Chicago and the one who was left or Dove to Detroit," said Donovan, after the draft was over.

We still had to sign Frazier. We had to convince him that he could play pro ball right away and finish his college education in the off-season. The first thing Donovan did was call Jack Hartman, the coach at Southern Illinois. Eddie did not want to do anything that would hurt Hartman.

Hartman told Eddie he was only interested in helping Frazier. If Frazier wanted to leave school and play pro ball, it was fine with him. No hard feelings. "I was living with my wife and son in a trailer near the campus at the time," recalled Frazier, who had been drafted by Denver of the ABA. "We weren't destitute, but if they wanted to think that, fine. Maybe they gave me more money because of it."

Pretty slick, eh? There were reports that his lawyer was talking in the neighborhood of $100,000. I know Frazier got good money, but as general manager of the Knicks I am not about to allow coach Holzman to reveal the amount. Let's just say everyone lived happily ever after. I hope so, anyway.

Walt made us happy from the moment he took his first dribble and made his first pass in training camp. Donovan and I watched McGuire put the boys through practice. I helped where I could. We were training at the McGuire Air Force Base for the first time. That was where Bradley was to be stationed after he finished the first part of his six-month tour down in Texas.

You could see Frazier had it. "Now we can put Cazzie in the corner and let the other guys worry about him a little," said McGuire, after getting Frazier. "Cazzie has proved he can score on anyone." It was all set. Frazier would open the season as a starter in the backcourt with Dick Barnett.

Those were the plans until Walt hurt his ankle in the second exhibition game. Frazier did not play his first regular season game until the Pistons came into the Garden on October 28, 1967. There were no standing ovations such as greeted Bradley when he broke in. There were no roars when Frazier hit his first few shots in practice.

People wanted to see Frazier because he was the first draft choice and he was great in the NIT, but he was no Bradley. So there was no unusual excitement when Walt was in the opening lineup for his first game in the NBA. McGuire assigned him to Dave Bing. "Bing is faster than Walker," explained Dick, who recognized Frazier's defensive quickness right away.

Walt did not get rave reviews after the game. "Walt Frazier looks like he can eventually make it," was the modest report in the *New York Post*. "He played well in his first start but made understandable mistakes. His shooting is off and he gets tired but he played seventeen encouraging minutes in the first half against Detroit. He had five assists, four rebounds and harassed Dave Bing enough to force a 3-for-12 opening half out of the fine Pistons' soph."

Frazier's second game was no better. It was in Oakland against San Francisco. He played fourteen minutes, shot 0-for-6 and had four assists. The Knicks lost their sixth straight and the only thing worth mentioning is that Jackson got thrown out for allegedly punching referee Bill Kunkel.

"He extended his arm and punched me in the side," insisted Kunkel, the ex-Yankee pitcher who later left the NBA to become an American League umpire. "Not only that, he called me a dirty so-and-so." Jackson had a different version, naturally. "I was knocked down," he said, "and when I got up and started to run downcourt, I ran into him. He must have misconstrued. I certainly wouldn't hit him intentionally."

There was another routine night for Frazier as Reed broke the losing streak in Los Angeles with his fifty-three points. Walt played sixteen minutes this time and did hit three of his four shots but didn't have an assist. He was having trouble. He couldn't capture the rhythm of the game. He was playing on the wrong RPMs. He was on 45, the game was on 78. In college, he was used to controlling the pace. In the pros, they press the ball and everything is accelerated. The twenty-four-second clock sees to that.

"I was afraid to shoot when I started," Frazier explained. "I'd take a shot and if I made it, I'd take another. If I didn't, I'd look too much to pass. Every time I missed, I could just hear the fans saying: 'Aw, hell, why is he shooting?'." Rookies have a tendency to do that. They think instead of playing. It changes when they get into the flow of things.

Frazier had his troubles. All the Knicks had troubles. Even Donovan when he decided he was going to join the team on the Coast and try to ease McGuire's tortured existence. I guess what happened to Eddie indicated the team was just snake-bitten, that's all.

Eddie cleared his desk but a complication arose. He got a toothache. The left side of his face was swollen and he had a lot of pain, so he called his dentist in New Jersey, where Eddie lived at the time. The dentist was out, and Eddie called another one.

That dentist told Eddie he had to leave at three o'clock. Eddie couldn't make it, so they made an appointment for 8:45 the next morning. That would give him plenty of time to make his helicopter connection from Newark to Kennedy to catch a noon plane to the Coast.

"Two teeth must come out," Donovan was told after

X-rays were taken. They came out and Eddie felt miserable. The weather was miserable, too. But Eddie was determined to make the flight. He wanted to get out to McGuire and see if he could help. He went back home to Elizabeth in plenty of time for the helicopter and found his wife, Marge, waiting with a message.

It was not good. "The chopper service called," she reported, "New York Airways said it canceled your 11:08 flight because of weather." You become accustomed to little inconveniences like that if you travel in the NBA. You learn how to get there no matter how many obstacles they put in your way. It costs players, teams and referees money in fines if you don't.

Eddie decided to catch a train to New York and then hop a cab to the airport. Mrs. Donovan drove him to the railroad station in Elizabeth just in time for him to miss the train. No problem. He grabbed a cab to Newark and caught a train there to New York.

He rushed upstairs and into a cab. "Take me to Kennedy Airport," he told the cabbie. "I've got to catch a noon plane." He made it by five minutes. He grabbed his two-suiter and ran to the boarding area. He was out of breath and out of a lot of blood from the tooth extractions, but he had made it.

At least he thought he had made it. He saw a sign. It read: "See the agent." Eddie went to see the agent. "Get on the bus and go to Newark," he was told. "We're not flying out of here because the weather is so bad." Airlines have a habit of springing little surprises like that on their passengers once in a while. Eddie is not one to discourage that easily. He went back to Newark and caught a 2:30 to the Coast.

Sometimes I wonder if the old railroad league wasn't better. We used planes when I first broke in, but not often. The league wasn't spread all over the country in those days. I guess nobody will ever forget the train ride from Rochester to play in Ft. Wayne.

All teams went through the same routine because there was only one train out of Rochester if you had to leave after the game to play in Ft. Wayne the next night. You would take a midnight sleeper and they would wake you up around five-thirty in the morning because you were getting off at Waterloo, Indiana, at six.

Then you would walk about a half-mile down the tracks until you came to a road that crossed over. You can imagine what a sight that must have been to the natives. Monsters with luggage that early in the morning must have looked like an invasion from Mars.

You would cross the tracks and walk to a little restaurant called The Green Parrot. You hammered on the door and woke up the proprietor. He arranged for cabs that drove you to Ft. Wayne. And some players complain today when the wine isn't cold enough on their first-class flights.

The teams chartered planes much more in those days. Today it rarely happens. The planes are too big and the traveling party is around sixteen or seventeen in pro basketball. Charters were used for short hops to Syracuse or Rochester from places like New York and Philadelphia. One year the Knicks decided to rent a charter for the season.

Fred Zollner, owner of the Pistons, had been flying his team around the league in his plane. The St. Louis Hawks figured it was worth the convenience to be able to leave when the team was ready. I know a lot of people who would like to have some of the hours back they have spent in airports.

So the Knicks hired a plane. It was nicknamed "Sputknick" after the first Russian satellite. It didn't last long.

A trip from New York to St. Louis took care of that. Fuzzy Levane was coaching the Knicks at the time. The plane got off okay and it was well on its way to the Midwest when the pilot decided to go back to the head. He left the copilot at the controls.

The pilot strolled back a few minutes later. He grabbed the handle of the door to the cockpit and pulled. It wouldn't budge. The door was locked. It locked automatically. He knew that but had forgotten to take the key with him.

It was impossible for the copilot to open the door because he could not reach it from his seat. He couldn't leave the controls. He was the only one up there. The pilot stuck his fingers into the crack of the door and tried to force it open. No good.

Trainer Don Freiderichs brought up his kit. He dug out surgical scissors. The pilot tried those. No good. Another guy brought up a beer can opener. No good. The pilot began to sweat. So did everyone else. "Now's the time to sell some insurance," a funny man whispered to Levane, who handled insurance on the side in those days.

It was hard to remain cool. Then the pilot really shook up the players. The weather had been bad all the time and there was a good chance the plane would have to make an emergency landing in the fog short of St. Louis. "It's too foggy in St. Louis," the pilot told Fuzzy, "and we may have to go in at Zanesville [Ohio]. We're not too far from there. I've got to get up front because the copilot has a probationary license. He is not allowed to land a plane in weather like this. I'm the only one who can."

Everyone went to work on that silly, little door, and they finally yanked it open. The plane did have to land in Zanesville, however. The Knicks rented cars and drove the rest of the way. Sputknick went up on waivers.

O
———
7

Things were getting a little better. Dick McGuire's stomach had settled down. So had the Knicks. Four victories in a row. Los Angeles, Seattle and two over San Diego. All on the road.

Seattle and San Diego were expansion teams, but the Knicks needed every victory they could get. Frazier still was trying to find himself. He had a 6-for-7 shooting game in Seattle and pulled down seven rebounds in twenty-one minutes. It was his best game to that point.

McGuire also decided to split up Bellamy and Reed. He wanted to see what would happen if Willis went back to center and Bells came off the bench to relieve. "Maybe Bellamy does better if he only plays twenty-five or thirty minutes," said McGuire after the 6-11 center shot 8-for-11 and grabbed nineteen rebounds in the first game with San Diego. "I don't know how you can play so long and not take more shots," said the Knick coach after Bells shot 0-for-2 in twenty minutes the next night.

That was Bellamy. Great at times. Especially when he played against Chamberlain and Russell. He had all the equipment and it was hard to believe he couldn't do it all the time. Maybe people expected too much of him.

I know it was that way when we got him from Baltimore. Everyone figured he was the real good big man the Knicks had been after for so many years. We almost had him when he first came into the league. He was eligible for the draft of 1960 and that year the Knicks had finished last with a 21-58 record.

We figured we had first crack at the draft. Bellamy was going to be our man, no doubt about that. It turned out we figured wrong. A Chicago franchise was being added and it was decided to give it the first draft choice.

There was a pretty good fight about that. The league explained that it wanted to give the new team a reasonable start with the first draft pick. Ned Irish argued that the Knicks had been around a long time and needed the kind of help Bellamy could supply. There were reports that Ned even threatened to quit the league if the Zephyrs got the first choice.

Bellamy went to Chicago and was a sensation his first year. Every time we looked at his statistics we got sick. He was second in scoring to Chamberlain with a 31.4 average and third to Wilt and Russell in rebounding with fifteen hundred in seventy-nine games. He was a standout in the all-star game and was named Rookie of the Year.

Five seasons later he finally put on a Knick uniform. We knew of his problems in Baltimore. They were well spread out in the papers. First with Buddy Jeannette when he was the coach. Then with Paul Seymour when he became coach and Jeanette moved up to general manager.

Bellamy was a holdout when Seymour took over as coach. Paul talked Jeanette into giving Bells a raise. Bellamy was too big and too good to give up on that easily. Seymour was fascinated by Walter's obvious talent. Who wouldn't be? And where could you find an available center like Bellamy, anyway?

Something happened that apparently made Seymour reevaluate. The Knicks were on the Coast when conversations started between Donovan and Jeannette. They knew the Knicks had been looking for a big man for years. They knew how badly Ned Irish had wanted Bellamy as a rookie. What would the Knicks give for him?

A lot of names were thrown around. The Knicks weren't interested in trading Reed or Van Arsdale or Stallworth or Komives. How about Barnes? Donovan had to think about that one. The Knicks were in the early stages of rebuilding and Bad News represented part of the young blood they had just obtained from the draft.

Barnes, Reed, Komives and Bryant had come out of the draft the year before and had given us a nice foundation. Bad News had been first draft choice and, boy, how we had sweated over that decision! That was the most unusual year I can ever remember in the draft. A lot of good players got out of college in 1964.

I was all over the map that year. My files really bulged. But it came down to Barnes, Reed and Luke Jackson as far as we were concerned. I showed Donovan all my material. We talked it over for hours and hours and we agreed that the three top players in the draft had to be Barnes, Reed and Jackson.

All we had to do was separate them. I had seen them all play for three years. Donovan had done some scouting himself. He was an excellent judge of talent. At the beginning I was watching other players. You don't really start scouting players when they are sophmores. I had been looking at Reed since he was a freshman but not really paying much attention to him. I went to Grambling to see Zelmo Beaty play with Prairie View, for instance.

I remember another time I saw Willis play in the NAIA

tournament in Kansas City. Now, there's a tournament!
You saw players and games until it came out of your ears.
Eight games a day for the first three or four days, starting
at ten in the morning. All the scouts would be there.
Marty Blake of St. Louis, Earl Lloyd of Detroit, George
Lee of San Francisco, Vince Miller of Philadelphia, Jerry
Colangelo of Chicago.

I'd get up around eight o'clock and get to the audi-
torium about 9:30. There would be four games. They'd
break for an hour and I'd go out with the fellows for a
sandwich. We'd come back and watch four more games
and then go to dinner.

There were thirty-two NCAA small colleges and they
would play every day for a week. I'd stay until I saw all
the teams and then leave. I saw Dick Barnett there the
first time he played. He was voted the Most Valuable
Player two straight years. He had that herky-jerky move
even then. Everyone knew he had the stuff to make it in
the pros.

Most of the time, when I would go to a college gym
nobody knew I was there. I didn't want to put any pressure on the players I was scouting. I would sneak in and
out. Sometimes I'd see two games in different cities on
the same day. One in the afternoon and the other at night.
I would fly to one city and then rent a car and cover the
area I had programmed for myself.

A lot of things can happen when you have traveled as
much as I did. One time in Alabama, I was driving a
rented car to the airport at Tuscaloosa. It was a dark,
rainy night on a dark, rainy road. Don't you know the car
broke down? I left the darn thing and began walking. It
was about a mile to a motel and I made it carrying my
luggage.

I went in for some coffee. I told the guy behind the
counter my sad story. He said he knew someone who was

going my way and arranged a ride. I wasn't thinking of anything but getting to the airport until my host, or hosts, arrived. They were two rough-looking characters and they had a beat-up old car.

We took off and I began thinking. I had on a good suit and was carrying expensive luggage and they were pretty mean looking. The rural roads were empty. We talked a little. I don't know what I said. But I was working myself up.

Then the car began to slow down. Could this be it? What a way for a nice Jewish boy to die. They started blinking the lights. I figured they were signaling. I thought I had had it. Then, out of the darkness, came a fellow. They greeted him. He hopped in and away we went. They had just stopped to pick him up on their way to work.

They dropped me off at the airport. They were real nice guys. You meet a lot of them when you travel. I don't know how many miles I did as a scout but I must have traveled enough to at least reach the moon.

Every year it wound up the same way. I would sit down with Donovan and go over my entire file with him. Barnes, Reed and Jackson gave me another idea. Films. It was nothing new. I always tried to get my hands on some films when I visited a school. They tell you so much. I still use them before almost every game we play.

I managed to get some films of games played by Jackson, Barnes and Reed. The college coaches, I found, always were very cooperative. I never met one that gave me a tough time. I remember once the coach even held up a game when I was late. I walked in and they escorted me to my seat down on the floor and everyone cheered.

That was a great thing for a guy who always tried to be as inconspicuous as possible. I felt as though I was sitting all alone in the middle of the floor at a Madison Square Garden sellout. But that was the kind of treatment I always got from the college people when they knew I was there.

They went out of their way to give us films when we needed them to help unravel the Barnes, Reed and Jackson situation. Those movies got more of a rerun than *Gone With the Wind*. Donovan and I ran them forward and backward until our eyeballs were imprinted with basketballs. We would have run the film sideways if it was possible.

We watched Reed play Jackson and Jackson play Barnes and Barnes play Reed. It was like boxing three numbers in the Double. We crisscrossed them and hoped we would come up with the winner. After all, they were only three players among hundreds coming out of school and it was strictly our judgment that they were the best. Or, at least, they were the ones we thought could help us the most.

Barnes was listed at 6-8 but we suspected he wasn't that tall. He was more like 6-7. But he could play forward and center. He was quick; much quicker than Jackson and Reed. He had a great physique. And he did look the best in the Olympic trials they held at St. John's.

Reed did not look good at all in those trials. That's where everyone, I think, made the mistake on Willis. I know we did. Reed was sick at the time and very weak. He never made the team. Barnes and Jackson did.

I guess there was less of an excuse for us than the others when we didn't take Reed in the first round. I'm sure we studied the three of them harder than anyone. Eddie and I never drank so much coffee or smoked so much in our lives. You could get instant emphysema just walking into the smog we created in Eddie's office.

We had to separate the players. Jackson and Reed were more alike. They were both big and strong and could shoot from outside, though Willis looked as though he could hit better. Jackson was a legitimate 6-9, but Reed did not appear to be 6-10.

Considerations like that are important, so I had Reed's height checked out one day. I called Red Thomas. He's an old buddy who is dean at Northwestern State College in Natchitoches, Louisiana. I used to go to all the games with him down there. Red went over to Grambling and had Reed measured. He told me Willis was about 6-9. Let's say closer to 6-8 than 6-10.

Even a little detail like that can make the difference when you are evaluating ballplayers. That was why I had come up with my work sheet. I hoped it would cover everything. It probably doesn't. Even now, I think of something I can add.

It's like a computer. You feed in all the material and hope it spits out the right answer. That's what Eddie and I did. I kept feeding him all the information I had compiled on Reed, Barnes and Jackson and we kept looking at the films for just a little more practical information.

It was tough. They all had size and poise and talent. We finally decided on Barnes. He had the quickness and strength and the game was becoming one of more speed every day. We figured Bad News would give height away to Chamberlain and Russell and Thurmond but would make it up with quickness. There was no one in the league Barnes's size who had his speed.

The Knicks had to be ready because they were picking first. Sometimes you can wait and make a decision on what's left. The way we were going in those days, we always seemed to be the first one at bat. When Commissioner Kennedy announced the draft was opened, we made it a little easier for those behind us by taking Barnes. We then sat back to see how fast Jackson and Reed went.

We did not wait long for the first surprise. Detroit, picking second, announced it was taking Joe Caldwell. He was a fine college ballplayer who had done well in the Olympics. Man, what speed. But people expected the Pistons to go for a center. They had Imhoff, who had been traded to them by the Knicks in 1962 for Gene Shue. And they had a seven-foot rookie named Reggie Harding who had played only high school ball.

Baltimore was next. We were sure Jackson or Reed would go now. The Bullets had Bellamy and Gus Johnson, but we figured they could use Willis or Luke to double up at forward and center. They picked Gary Bradds, a lanky player out of Ohio State.

Could we be that far off on our ratings? It was possible. The Knicks had made some picks in the past that turned out to be questionable. There never is any guarantee that you are right just because you think you are. But we still could not understand why Jackson and Reed weren't being grabbed. Not that we were rooting for it to happen.

Philadelphia was next. It had to happen now. Johnny Kerr wasn't getting any younger at center. Connie Dierking was the backup man. The 76ers had to take Willis or Luke. They did. They announced Jackson.

There were only four teams left. Los Angeles had made Walt Hazzard of UCLA a territorial choice and that was its first-round pick. The Lakers really did not need a guard that much. They had Jerry West, Dick Barnett, Frank Selvy and Jim King. But Hazzard was a local hero and Selvy was retiring.

It now was St. Louis's turn. Ben Kerner, my old boss, was a shrewd man. So was Marty Blake, who did all the scouting for the Hawks. They had enough size in Beaty and Bridges. They still had Cliff Hagan and Gene Tormohlen and Mike Farmer. All workable players.

We never figured the Hawks would go for Reed. They needed a big scoring guard too much. They got one. They chose Jeff Mullins of Duke. It's funny when you look back and see what happened to some of the players who were drafted. A fellow like Mullins, who wound up doing such great things in San Francisco. Or a player like Caldwell, who had done so much for the Hawks after being traded by Detroit.

San Francisco had the same problem as St. Louis. It needed a guy with size in the backcourt who could shoot. The Warriors still had Chamberlain and Thurmond playing on the same team. They figured Tom Meschery, Wayne Hightower and George Lee, with Thurmond, could handle the forward problems adequately.

The trouble was in the backcourt. Guy Rodgers and Al Attles were quick but not big. So the Warriors chose Barry Kramer of NYU. There was a hot discussion at the San Francisco table before the decision was made. Eddie Gottlieb, still working as an advisor out there, preferred to take the best man available and not pick to a position. That's how the Warriors wound up with Thurmond remember? Gotty lost this time.

Two more to go. First Cincinnati, which had finished second in the East with a better record than San Francisco, which had won in the West, and then Boston, the NBA champ. We got over that one. The Royals went for George Wilson, a local player out of the University of Cincinnati.

Boston was last. It had no serious manpower problems. Red Auerbach had Bill Russell, still in his prime, John Havlicek, Tommy Heinsohn, Sam Jones, K.C. Jones, Tom Sanders and Willie Naulls. He was looking for someone to make up for the retirements of Frank Ramsey and Jim Loscutoff.

But he had no real sweat. Red had the class of the league. They still were holding the championship spot in the NBA's official guide for the Boston team picture. So when it came time for Auerbach to pick for the Celtics, he had no pressure and an open mind. He took seven-foot Mel Counts. He had a reason. "I think Counts will be a good forward, the way he shoots," said Auerbach. "Just imagine. A seven-foot forward."

Reasonable. Great from Red's viewpoint. Any pick you decide on always makes sense to you. Otherwise you wouldn't make it. The Knicks had made a lot of selections that made sense to them but didn't turn out well.

Every team has a history of errors. There is no one who is right all the time. I'm sure if Auerbach and the others had to do it all over again, knowing what they know now, they would have taken Reed faster than you can say Willis Reed.

When they didn't, and Reed was still alive as we led off the second round, we really couldn't believe it. That didn't make us any smarter than the next guy. We could have been wrong as we had been wrong many times before. We had made a mistake about Reed, ourselves, when you look back at things.

Why didn't we pick him first? A good question. Barnes was the biggest influence. We just rated him a little higher. We learned better. We also learned another thing about scouting big men in an all-star game, such as the Olympic trials.

I knew Willis was a big, strong kid with a great attitude. I thought he ran well for a big horse who could shoot outside. But he did not do well in the Olympic trials. I must confess that was an influence in our decision. We failed to consider that the big man is at a disadvantage in college all-star games. He gets the ball last. The ball is controlled by the guards and then the forwards. They know the scouts are watching and it might mean money if they are high in the draft. They are out to increase their value. A big man hasn't got much of a chance under those conditions.

There are very few superguarantees in the draft. I can't name many. There were Chamberlain and Oscar Robertson and Lew Alcindor. That's about all. Everyone knew they could come right in and do it. West? He had to sit on the bench when he broke in and Freddie Schaus, who had coached him at West Virginia, was his coach in Los Angeles. You know about Cousy.

Bill Russell? Never. No one dreamed he would step into the NBA and do the things he did. He had good credentials at San Francisco University. He was the key man on a team that featured defense. Yet Kerner made a deal to draft him and trade him to Boston before he even played a game for the St. Louis Hawks. For a very good reason. It helped his franchise become successful. That's the name of the game.

You have to give Red Auerbach and Walter Brown credit for some vision. They saw something vital in Russell and were even willing to wait for him to compete in the Olympics and report late to the team. In fact, Bill played in only forty-eight games for the 1956-57 Celtics, but they won the championship, anyway.

Auerbach covers the subject of Russell very well in the book he did with Paul Sann of the *New York Post*. He tells of how he canvassed all his basketball friends for an opinion. Fred Scolari, who played for Red with the Washington Caps, provided the clincher. "Red, this kid can't shoot to save his ass," Fat Freddie told Auerbach. "He can't hit the side of the basket. He's only the greatest basketball player I ever saw."

That did it. Red went to Les Harrison, my old boss in Rochester, and tried to make a deal. He wanted Les, picking first, to take Russell for Boston. That didn't work. Kerner was next because St. Louis was picking second. Auerbach offered Easy Ed Macauley, a St. Louis Univer-

sity star who wanted to go back home because he had a
sick youngster. "You got a deal," Ben told Auerbach.

Kerner, as I've said, was a shrewd man. He sensed that
Auerbach really must want Russell awfully badly to give
up an all-star center like Macauley. "There's only one little
thing," Kerner told Auerbach. "You got the rights to Cliff
Hagan when he comes out of the army, and I can use him,
too. You're getting Frank Ramsey and Tommy Heinsohn
and you got that gorilla Jim Loscutoff in the corner, right?
So you give me Hagan with Macauley and you get Russell
and we're even up."

The Knicks have been down that street. It happened
in the deal we made with Baltimore for Bellamy. And it
happened in the deal we made with Detroit for Dave
DeBusschere. You simply have to make up your mind that
you are getting value. If you want a player badly enough,
you are prepared to give a little more for him. Let's face it,
you start every deal with the idea of taking advantage of
the other guy, anyway.

I sometimes wonder what would have happened in St.
Louis if Kerner had kept Russell. Would St. Louis have
moved to Atlanta? Would Kerner have sold the franchise?
Benny, a hardworking guy, got out with a lot of money
and deserved it. I remember all those nights he would be
in his office, until midnight sometimes, trying to make pro
basketball profitable in St. Louis.

He did get a break when he came up with Bob Pettit.
It was a break. Baltimore picked first that year and took
Frank Selvy, a great shooting guard from Furman. That
left Pettit. He was from L.S.U. and, in those days, the
basketball down there didn't exactly excite anyone.

Kerner was excited. He was losing a lot of money in
Milwaukee at that time. He desperately needed someone
with an image like Pettit. He realized Bob would be ex-

pensive because AAU ball was big, then, and there were stories that Pettit preferred to play for an industrial team and get started on a business career.

So Pettit joined Milwaukee, and Kerner turned him over to a young coach named Red Holzman. That was in 1954. I wonder whatever became of Pettit? Let's put it another way. He lasted a helluva lot longer with Kerner than I did. That's what I keep saying. Kerner was a very shrewd man.

To each his own mistake. Today, you can look back and say Reed was a mistake and Barnes was a mistake. Willis thought it was when he didn't go on the first round. He didn't believe Donovan when Eddie called and told him that he had been picked by the Knicks but on the second round.

Maybe taking Barnes first was a mistake and we were just plain lucky. We'll take it that way. It worked out, didn't it? Bad News was the player Baltimore really wanted when we went after Bellamy. The Knicks would have preferred to substitute someone older. But Baltimore insisted.

It was decided. Johnny Green, John Egan, Barnes and a little cash. The Knicks were on their way home from California when the deal was concluded. Donovan rushed to the airport to break the news. It was hardly the place. Some people might even say it was kind of cruel. But there was a reason.

A deal like that can never be kept a secret. Someone is bound to find out and break it, and then the player gets mad. He's right. He should be told first. He should not find out he is going to another team in a newspaper or on radio or television. That is why Donovan met the plane.

He told Green and Barnes and Egan in the airport that they belonged to Baltimore. None of them liked it. They wanted to play in New York. But Donovan had seen the opportunity finally to get a big man who would give the Knicks a chance against Chamberlain and Russell.

Eddie was aware of Bellamy's problems. He felt New York might help Bells and Bells might help New York. He knew he was taking a calculated risk in switching Reed to forward. Willis was a natural center. But we all agreed that Willis had a great attitude and was willing to do anything, even play out of position.

There are times when you just have to be in the right place at the right time. Maybe if we had not drafted Bad News Barnes, we wouldn't have gotten Bellamy. Then we wouldn't have had Bellamy to get Dave DeBusschere.

8

"Just think," said Dick McGuire in one of his droll moments. "I might be sitting on the bench with Bill Bradley on one side and Cazzie Russell on the other."

That was just like McGuire. He was trying to laugh off the situation. It wasn't long before I was on the bench and sitting near me were Bradley and Russell for my first game in the old Garden against the Los Angeles Lakers.

I had two days to get ready. As far as I was concerned, the Knicks were starting a new season. They had to learn a new offense. I was adding the press. St. Louis had given us a lot of trouble with it. I had seen that.

I felt the only way to learn how to work against it was to learn how to do it. I was surprised the way the players caught on so fast. We had some kind of bonus in Phil Jackson. He knew how to press well. His college team at North Dakota had used it a lot. He knew how to harass. He had the long arms and the reach.

Frazier wasn't playing that much and I wanted to get him involved more. I wanted the team playing together more. I wanted some type of self-discipline. I wanted no more than any other coach wants. The team was down and I was asked to pick it up.

A lot of people ask me how I made a team out of the Knicks. What was my recipe? "The same way Selma makes chicken in the pot," I tell them. They think I'm kidding but I'm serious. Listen.

"Buy a chicken, three and a half to four pounds," says Selma. "It should be a big chicken. It should serve four but in our house it serves two because we're big eaters. Have the butcher cut it into eighths. Boil some water. Put the chicken in a bowl and pour the boiling water over it. Strain it and clean the remaining refuse off the chicken.

"Put the chicken in a pot of cold water that barely covers the chicken. Add two tablespoons of salt and bring the water to a boil. Skim off the fat. Put in four or five carrots and four celery stalks with the greens on top. Add two onions, a parsnip and a root. The root is very important. A turnip is optional. So is a bay leaf.

"Now, cook on a soft boil, half-covered so the steam comes out. Cook about an hour and then add some dills and a few stems of parsley. Very important. You might have to add a little more water if it is thick soup and the water has boiled down. Cook another half hour. The dill and parsley should give it a nice aroma and the chicken should be meaty."

Making chicken-in-the-pot is like making a team. It's the personal touch. As Selma would say: "It's hard to give a recipe because you have to season and cook to your own taste." The same with basketball. The same with the Knicks.

I had my own recipe and I had to season to my own taste. I wasn't going to be in any hurry. I was going to soft boil everything until the team was ready. That is why I started with fundamentals. It is easier for the players to understand when you go back to basics.

79

The Knicks did remarkably well in the two days I had before we faced the Lakers. We lost that game and the next one to Cincinnati, but I was encouraged. It was now six straight defeats for the Knicks and two for me. "I suppose the tendency would be to say: 'Why does this have to happen to me?' " I said when asked. "But I'm the kind of guy who doesn't worry about what's already past. If the train's gone when I get there, it's gone."

I guess I startled a few people when we lost to Cincinnati in the Garden. They thought I was crazy when I took out Bellamy and Reed with four minutes to go and put in Nate Bowman and Phil Jackson. We were behind, 114–105, at the time and I had to do something. I also was building confidence. I wanted all the players to feel they had to be ready all the time. There was no situation where I would be afraid to use them.

I laughed when I read some of the comments after the game. "I didn't think I was tired, but maybe the coach saw something I wasn't aware of," said Reed. "Why do you think he did that?" Coach Ed Jucker asked his Cincinnati players. "Someone has to sacrifice," observed Oscar Robertson. "Sometimes the best players on the floor don't make the best team."

The Big O sure is smart. He read it perfectly. The team we had on the floor was not doing the job defensively. Otherwise, would we be behind by nine? Another thing. I like to do something, almost anything, to make the other team change if it is doing things right. There are times when I deliberately create a mismatch and hope it will cause the other team to concentrate on beating it.

Basketball is a team game and if you can interrupt the team pattern, you have a better chance. It's like the little trick we used in the schoolyard when we shot fouls for money. If a guy was extremely hot you, as the retriever, would roll the ball off to a side so that the shooter would have to get off his spot. That way you break his concentration and hope to cool him off.

That is why I have no fear about playing Bill Bradley against a Mel Counts, for example. Counts towers over Bill, is a great shooter and has had some fine nights against the Knicks. But if the team wants to go to Counts all night, that's fine with us. All strategy is great if you have a team that can play and win. If not, it's worth about as much as yesterday's news.

The Knicks finally won one for me in Philadelphia, where it probably was least expected. We hadn't beaten the 76ers on their court in three seasons. I can't really tell you what happened on offense. I rarely can. I spend most of my time checking defensive positions. I feel if the players are positioned right on defense, everything else will work out. The offense is easy after that.

I know I drove the Philadelphia fans nuts with my yelling. I had told the players we were going to press the 76ers. We were going to harass their ball handlers and make them work hard to bring the ball down. That meant we had to work hard. Me, too.

As soon as the game started, I was out in front of the bench, screaming: "Pick up . . . Face the ball, Cazzie . . . Hurry up, Bellamy . . . Get up there, Jackson, know where the ball is . . . Help out, Willis . . . Chase 'em now, chase 'em . . . C'mon, Bellamy . . . Be ready, Frazier . . . Willis, pick up Will . . . Get at 'em, Frazier . . . Get up ahead, Barnett . . . Don't let 'em get that close, Van."

It was all about defense. You always get the feeling that the first time you don't mention it, something goes wrong. I had only one voice to give to the team. I was hoping that someday the bench would join in and then we would have it made. I had to do all the yelling at the start.

Alex Hannum heard me all the way down at his end of the floor. "I heard him yelling: 'Go get 'em, go press 'em,' "

81

the 76er coach acknowledged. "You've got to say something for Red and their dedication."

Chamberlain was impressed. He had been saying all along that the Knicks had the material to play better. So had Bill Russell and the Boston Celtics. "They were just fantastic," said Wilt after the Knicks had snapped a nine-game winning streak for the 76ers. "This is the type of game they should play all the time. They are capable of it and I tell that to Bellamy all the time."

The Knicks were happy but still skeptical. They had done this before and then losing had set in. "It remains to be seen if we continue this hustling defense every game," suggested Dick Van Arsdale. "If we keep pressing like this, I'll have to go to Dr. Barnard for a new heart," said Butch Komives.

We continued to press and we began to win and Komives did not need a transplant. We rolled to six straight victories and I still had not used Bradley. He was sitting on the bench alongside me and rooting. We had put him on the disabled list and he was due to come back when we left on my first Coast trip.

We made it five in a row in San Diego, where I came face-to-face with my first tough decision as coach. I had spoken to Donovan back in New York and Bradley was going back on the roster at our next stop, Los Angeles. Someone had to go and I had to tell him. We were forty-five games into the season and everyone had worked so hard.

It probably was a tougher decision for Donovan than me. The player we were going to drop was Freddie Crawford. With Bradley coming back to the backcourt, we had three big guards—Bill, Frazier and Barnett. There just was no room for Crawford. I know how hard it must have been for Donovan, but sports is like that. Always hard decisions; little time for sentiment.

Donovan had been Crawford's coach at St. Bonaventure when Freddie and Tom Stith came down with tuberculosis. Eddie knew the struggle Crawford made to come back and play college ball again. He knew what it meant to Freddie if he could play pro ball, so Eddie drafted him in 1966 but he didn't make it in training camp.

Crawford got the first call when a spot was available. He was pulled back from the Eastern League and got into nineteen games that season. He was even the high scorer in the one game the Knicks took from the Celtics in the 1966-67 playoffs. He had great desire and played hard and had the ideal attitude. But he was the thirteenth man in our situation and we could only carry twelve.

I asked Danny Whelan to have Freddie come to my room at the Mission Valley Inn in San Diego. You always rehearse what you're going to say at a time like that. Then you never say it exactly that way. I simply explained that Bradley was coming back and we had to drop him. We were sorry and we would like to keep him but it was impossible.

Nobody likes to do things like that, especially to a fine boy like Crawford. We really thought he belonged in the league and could help a lot of teams. It turned out that way. But I know how badly he must have felt to get the news all the way out there in San Diego and then have to go all the way back to New York alone.

We only played Bradley four minutes that first night he was reactivated in Los Angeles. I had no intention of rushing him. As long as we were winning, he might have sat on the bench forever. We were not only winning, but I liked the way it was happening. The guys were getting the hang of the press and team defense. They were helping out and enjoying it.

There is nothing like results. We were cutting down the shots by the other team. We were harassing them into mistakes or misses. "I had my shots," said Elgin Baylor after he went 2-for-18 in forty-three minutes. He still could not believe the Knicks had anything to do with it.

But there was solid evidence that the defense was growing and here we had played only eight games. Los Angeles had gotten only 74 shots, Philadelphia 89, Chicago 89, Detroit 87, San Diego 85 and only Seattle 101. That was our six-game winning streak and the players began to understand why. "They seem to be playing together as a team," Baylor did admit.

I had no set ideas about players at the time. I was ready to use anyone at anytime. I wanted to keep the pressure on the other team and I didn't want any tired players on the floor. I was ad-libbing, you might say. The game situation had something to do with it, of course.

In the game with Los Angeles, I know I must have surprised everyone early in the fourth quarter. We were leading by three and I had Frazier, Jackson, Bradley, Cazzie and Reed on the floor to protect it. Bradley only played four minutes in the game, all at that time. We went off on a 13–2 tear and put it away.

Frazier was beautiful for the first time. He took Archie Clark right out of the game after he had gotten off to a hot start. Walt was more aggressive. He was positive and no longer uncertain. He grabbed seven rebounds and got off some great passes while getting eight assists. He also shot 5-for-9. I remember Nate Bowman after the game. "That's the way to go," he hollered across the room to Frazier. "You're our Johnny Unitas."

I could feel the team growing right there and Bowman was to help a lot with his cheerleading. Nate came to the Knicks a little angry at the other teams who never gave him a chance to play. But life isn't always pleasant for everybody, and I guess Bowman had to fight to get where he was. We all have a tendency, anyway, of criticizing the other guy's hangups but forgetting we also have some. Who's perfect?

Bowman did his job very well for the Knicks. No one yelled louder from the bench or screamed more at the officials and other players. No one worked harder in practice. He was the ringleader of the Minutemen, our reserves, in every scrimmage with the starters.

I would have to say that Bowman best symbolized the team spirit and involvement of the Knicks. He would play his five or ten minutes with the same determination of a Reed. He was only a thousand-dollar-waiver claim by Donovan, but was worth a lot to me and the Knicks when he was with us.

I don't know who it was, but someone decided it would be fun to give a game-ball to the player who did the most ridiculous thing. It might have come from Cazzie, who is full of ideas like that. Or maybe even Riordan, since we didn't start the award until Mike had joined the team for the 1968-69 season.

Bowman wound up winning it most of the time; generally on shots that missed the basket or rolled off his hand. Nate usually took it as a big joke. Once in a while he would get upset and insist someone else deserved it. What the prize really did was help establish togetherness. A team that lives together and plays together should laugh and even argue together.

A nice thing happened to Dick Barnett while we were in Los Angeles. He received word that he had made the all-star team for the first time. They finally recognized what we on the Knicks knew all the time—Barnett was an outstanding basketball player. He was drafted by Syracuse in 1959, the year we took Johnny Green as our first choice, and he was just made an all-star.

I had seen Dick play many times but the people in New York had not seen him until he walked into the Garden one night in the fall of 1959. They never will forget him. He was the first of the mod dressers. Mod, in those days, was a little different than today, but Barnett still is the stylist on the Knicks.

This particular night he really floored everyone in his debut. He walked in with a Chesterfield coat, homburg, striped pants, spats and an umbrella hooked on his arm. Everyone knew he was there. They still know he is there, and it is now eleven years later. I am sure they appreciate him more. I know I do.

He was always tagged as a great shooter. But he's an awfully smart player. He's not given nearly enough credit for knowing a lot about the game. Everyone always said he was a great shooter and then they'd stop. But I never thought it ended there. Not if you watched him as much as I did.

Barnett just happened to be in the wrong places at the right time. When he was picked by Syracuse, he wound up with a team that had Larry Costello, Hal Greer, Al Bianchi and Paul Seymour. He got tired of sitting on the bench, so when the American Basketball League was formed, he jumped for more money and a chance to play. That was in 1961.

He got his chance to play but the "more money" wasn't there. His team, the Cleveland Pipers, won the championship and what do you think his share was? He got a check for seventeen dollars. "I never told anyone on the team about it," explained Barnett. Why? "I didn't want them to feel bad that I was the only one getting paid."

Dick was back in the NBA the next season. Los Angeles bought the rights from Syracuse. Once more he walked into a tough situation. The Lakers were loaded at guard. Dick did get to start when West got hurt. Otherwise he was used to come off the bench. His playing time dwindled in each of his three seasons in Los Angeles.

86

We knew this. Eddie Donovan never wasted any time as general manager. He was in constant touch with the other teams. He held conversations. He built bridges. He discussed conditions and personnel with general managers.

Freddie Schaus was looking around for some insurance behind Elgin Baylor. The injuries were coming faster and faster for Ol' Elg and Schaus did not want to get caught short. We were looking for someone to replace Art Heyman.

Eddie and I agreed that Barnett would be perfect. Dick wanted a chance to play more and we could give it to him. "Every place I've been, I've had to play behind someone," Dick had said many times. "I'd like a chance to be out front just once."

Los Angeles was happy to take Bob Boozer. We had gotten Boozer in a three-way deal with Cincinnati and Detroit. The Pistons sent us Johnny Egan, we sent Donnie Butcher and Bob Duffy to them and they shipped Larry Staverman to Cincy. It also cost us a little cash but it was the first of many moves that were to be vital to the making of the Knicks.

Boozer and Egan both contributed while they were with New York. Then Boozer was used to get Barnett, and Egan was part of the deal that brought Bellamy. Call it luck or whatever but we seemed to improve with every change that was made since 1964, the year of that great draft.

Nobody, not even knowledgeable New York fans, really appreciated Barnett until he played for the Knicks. I know this: nobody appreciates him more than I do. He made the job of putting in a new defense a lot easier. That's because he has such great basketball instinct. He grasps things faster than anyone.

He doesn't say much but he has a quiet sense of humor. "Red," he'll say, "I don't know if you're conning me or

I'm conning you." He is an amazing young man. Young compared to me, that is. He is never out of shape. No one works harder.

Ask him why and you will get a simple answer: "Money." He likes the stuff almost as much as he likes basketball. He has to like basketball the way he plays it. There is no other way to explain how hard he worked to get back after tearing an Achilles tendon late in the 1966-67 season.

He missed the playoffs with Boston because of the accident. He already was back home in Los Angeles getting ready to begin the rehabilitation program set up by Dr. Yanigasawa. The doc was a great surgeon. He performed all operations on the Knicks and Rangers. One on Donovan and one on me, too.

That was a funny one. Eddie was down the beach with his kids. "Last one in is a rotten egg," one of them yelled. They raced into the water and Eddie tore his Achilles tendon. Just like Barnett.

Barnett went home to Coast and worked all summer on strengthening his ankle, heel and leg. He ran on the beach every day. He lifted weights. When the 1967-68 training camp opened, Barnett was there, running like a rookie. You would never believe he had suffered the kind of injury that had shortened the careers of many athletes.

Take Luke Jackson, for example. He had the same injury and had a lot more trouble. Of course, Luke's problem was complicated by an artery blockage that caused them to dig a divot in the back of his leg, just below the calf. Too bad. A fine ballplayer.

Yet it only goes to show how much luck is involved. Suppose we had taken Jackson over Barnes in the 1964 draft and he had missed most of the 1968-69 and 1969-70 seasons for us. Or suppose Jackson had not gotten hurt, would Boston have beaten Philadelphia in the 1968-69 playoffs? And if Philadelphia had won and gone on to capture the NBA championship for the second straight year, would Wilt Chamberlain have wanted to be traded to Los Angeles?

You just never know about things like that, do you?

9

"Cazzie! Cazzie! Wrong way, Cazzie!" I screamed. I couldn't believe it. Cazzie had taken the tap and was headed in the wrong direction.

It happened shortly after we had our winning streak broken at six in San Francisco. In fact, we lost two in a row after that and we were in Baltimore, trying to avoid three. Dick Van Arsdale had grabbed the tap to start the fourth period and passed to Cazzie. He streaked for the wrong basket. The ball bounced off his leg and out of bounds, so we will never really know if he was going to shoot.

The dialogue in the dressing room after the game was hysterical. Especially since we won by only two points, 111–109. "I knew I was going the wrong way," Caz insisted. "I heard Red screaming. I wasn't going to shoot."

Em Bryant gave Cazzie one of those you-gotta-be-kidding looks. "No, you weren't going to shoot," he said to Cazzie. "You were in a squat, already." The players laughed. "Look here," Russell shouted to everyone. "Do you really think I was going to shoot that ball? Shame on you."

Walt Frazier looked up. "You didn't about face with it, you know," he suggested with a straight face. "Believe me, I wouldn't have shot it," Cazzie persisted. "They lined up wrong for the tap, anyway." That led to an argument between Reed and Bradley and enabled Cazzie to sneak away.

It was a good sign. The players were having fun. They were enjoying each other. Of course, winning helps. By now Bradley was back in full swing and was getting a lot of action, along with Cazzie, Van Arsdale, Barnett and Reed. The team was coming on. We weren't winning that often but our defense, especially the press, was maturing.

Frazier still was working only about eighteen minutes a game but you could see the improvement. I liked the way he harassed Earl Monroe down in Baltimore. Little did I know that it was going to be the start of something big in the NBA—Frazier vs. Monroe. A few nights later in Detroit, he helped cool off Dave Bing and Eddie Miles. I used him twenty-eight minutes that night and made up my mind he was going to play more, a lot more, after the all-star break.

We were 23-28 going into the 1968 all-star game, which the East took from the West, 144–124, in the Garden. Our man, Barnett, distinguished himself, as we expected, with 7-for-12 in twenty-two minutes. So did Reed, with 7-for-14 and eight rebounds in twenty-five minutes.

Just about that time, they announced that there would be expansion the following season. Milwaukee and Phoenix were coming into the league. The Knicks didn't like it. They fought it. It was no time for us to give up any of our players.

The strength of our team was its depth. We had suffered so many years and had struggled to rebuild. Now that we were getting someplace, we would be losing three players and one of our first eight. We would be able to protect only seven, and that was more of a problem for us than the other teams.

I didn't like it at all. I didn't like the anxiety it would create among the players when the guessing game started —and it started right away. I didn't like the idea of working hard to establish a team defense and offense and then losing a valuable part.

I was freewheeling at the time. There would be games where nine players would play sixteen minutes or more. They were getting so good, there were times they didn't need me around. One night they proved it. I got thrown out of my first Knick game as a coach, Reed took over and we won.

It was our first home game in seventeen days. We had just come off a ten-game trip and were playing San Francisco, without Nate Thurmond. I got two technicals and that is an automatic out in the NBA. Only the second belonged to me. I got the other trying to protect Reed.

He and LaRusso were at it, again. I guess Willis never forgot the punch Rudy threw the year before. This time, Reed threw an elbow and LaRusso was decked. I was on my feet screaming at the refs about getting that guy off Willis's back. It was partly a smokescreen. I wanted to distract the refs, if I could.

It got me a technical with 2:43 to go in the third period. With 2:43 to go in the fourth, I got the second and it was that LaRusso again. This time they gave him a continuation basket and I didn't like the call. Earl Strom called both 'Technicals' and gave me the signal I was out. I appointed Reed the coach.

"What do you want me to run?" asked Willis, taking the job very seriously. I told him to do whatever he wanted with the team. One guy suggested he should sell it. Willis coached the hell out of those remaining minutes. He called time with six seconds left and us leading by three points. He wanted to warn the guys about a three-pointer.

He was smart. I know everyone thinks the pros should be aware of things like that all the time. But it just doesn't work that way. You have to keep reminding players. You never take anything for granted. When it gets down to the nitty-gritty stage of a game, the safest thing to do is call time and discuss the situation.

That is why I try to save some of my times-out for the closing minute or so. I don't want to get caught without one if I can help it. They are better to have than not to have. Sometimes they do not help, even when you think you have used one properly.

I remember one Knick game with Philadelphia in the Garden. I'm not going to mention the player because I don't want to embarrass him. But a time-out was called with the Knicks leading by three points and only a few seconds to go. "No foul, no three-pointer," everyone was cautioned in the huddle.

The words still were ringing when this player pressed Hal Greer as he fired a long jumper. There was contact, the shot went in, Greer got a free throw, made it and sent the game into overtime. The 76ers won, of course. To this day that Knick player insists he did the right thing by trying to make the shot tough for Greer.

It's not like the old days, though. Les Harrison was our owner and coach in Rochester and we called a time-out mostly to rest. We had no such things as plays. It was all ad-lib style, the kind of things we ran in the schoolyard and in college. You know: give-and-go, change-of-direction, running your man into picks.

Les did know talent. He knew that the ballplayers with the most finesse came from the East. He stocked the club with ball handlers mostly from around New York and got his size from the Midwest and South. We had a built-in togetherness, but Les had his own little way of helping.

He was great for keeping the guys happy. He was good getting them together when we were losing. He would do anything for them. If things were going badly, he'd say: "C'mon, we'll have dinner and then we'll go to the hotel and have a pinochle tournament."

We'd play pinochle and he'd send down for sandwiches. I guess he always felt a team travels on its stomach. I remember when we played preseason games and we would travel by car.

Arnie Johnson, Bobby Wanzer, Les and I would be in one car and Les would suggest we have a cookout. Arnie was a good cook. We'd stop and Les would buy steaks and things and we'd eat up a storm. Those were the days when we got four dollars meal money. Today the guys in the NBA get nineteen dollars a day, the highest in sports. Of course, in those days we drank two-cents plain. Today, the players drink Chablis or Pouilly Fuissé.

My first time on the road with Rochester, instead of Les giving us meal money, he told us to eat anything we wanted at the hotel and sign. Everyone loaded up. That was the last time. It was four dollars a day after that, except for the cookouts and the sandwiches with the pinochle game.

I learned a lot from Les. He showed me that a coach could be involved with his players up to a point. He taught me that basketball could be enjoyable and not torture. He demonstrated that there could be communication and dialogue between the coach and players—but the players must be ready to play at all times.

I don't mind springing for a beer or a meal. I enjoy fooling around with the players at the proper time. The only line I draw is when we hole up at a motel. I insist that the players be roomed away from the coach, the

94

trainer and the newspapermen. On another floor, always.

I think the players are entitled to that freedom. I believe they would like to roam in and out without running into me or Danny Whelan or the newspapermen who travel with us. I think it is hard enough playing, practicing and traveling and they have earned the right to relax any way they want in their off-hours. There is no such thing as a bed check.

It is their money and their lives. They can do with it what they want. All the Garden asks is that they remain aware of their responsibilities and do what they are being paid for. Pro basketball is a demanding sport—the most demanding—and the most important commodity is time.

That is what I'm interested in—time. The Garden people are devoting their time, Whelan is devoting his time, the fans are devoting their time, the newspapermen are devoting their time, so why not the players? Time is just about the only thing I am strict about.

I don't think it is fair for everyone to be sitting on a bus waiting for one guy. I don't think it is right for all the players to be on time for practice and one guy to stroll in late. You have to make the players believe that you cannot waste time. If you are irresponsible about time, you will be irresponsible about playing. Irresponsibility breeds more irresponsibility.

We have made a joke of our little fines on the Knicks. I remember once, however, when it wasn't very funny to Bellamy. He had this habit of hooking onto a telephone in every airport. If we were leaving New York, he was on the phone and the last one on the plane. If we were coming home, he was still on the phone and the last one on the plane.

Not like Bowman. He always was the first aboard because he wanted the front seat on the aisle so he could stretch his legs. Bells didn't care. He must have owned stock in the telephone company.

In some airport, I forget which one, Bellamy was on the phone as usual. I swear he was no more than one hundred feet way from the boarding area when last seen. But when we got on the plane, and they closed the door, there was no Bellamy. He was left behind. It cost him the price of the flight and a fifty dollar fine. That was the biggest fine I ever levied, but it was automatic so I really had nothing to do with it. Bellamy paid with no argument or explanation. I'm sure it was his most expensive phone call. Or was it?

Bells always had good taste. He dressed and ate and lived well. He bought a big home in Baltimore where and his wife Helen stayed while he was playing for New York. He knew how to spend money as, for example, on a trip to Evansville when McGuire had the team.

The men left from New York in bad weather. They had to go to St. Louis and change there for a plane to Lexington for a connection to Evansville. When they arrived at the airport in Kentucky, there were not enough seats on the commercial flight to Evansville.

Someone got the bright idea of hiring a fleet of Piper Cubs. The investigation started. Sure enough, the Knicks could rent private planes to get them to the game on time. Bellamy had wandered over to hear Frankie Blauschild negotiate. "How much is a plane?" Bells asked the guy behind the counter. "One hundred and seventy-five dollars," was the answer. "I'll take one," said Bellamy.

Only two planes were necessary. An advance guard went out on them. The others were able to go commercial because seats opened up at the last minute.

Bradley probably will remember Evansville . . . or the night before in Cincinnati. I never put him in the game against the Royals. Someone pointed out that it probably was the first time Bill had ever been benched. I never thought of that, really. He had been going bad and I wanted him to pull himself together.

He wasn't the only one going bad. We were not winning enough. We were hanging around five games or so under .500 and that was not good. I figured most of the pressure was on Bradley. I wanted him to sit and watch a game, even if it meant blowing it.

We won it, thanks to Cazzie and a few other things. Cazzie hit one of his clutch shots with nothing left in overtime. He was on a hot streak at the time. We weren't winning much but our defense was getting better. I noticed it. So did other people.

"We take pride in our defense," said Johnny Kerr, then coaching Chicago. "But the Knick defense is tougher than ours. We are not as aware as the Knicks. We don't anticipate like they do." Then there was Guerin. "There is tremendous improvement in the Knicks," said Richie. "They challenge you all over on defense now."

Those things were encouraging. Not that I needed it. No one could tell better than I that the players were more aware on defense. I like that word "aware." I think that's the key to everything—awareness. If some scientist could figure a way to bottle it and inject everyone with it, what an interesting world it would be.

The other teams were becoming more aware of our players. Eddie Donovan was getting more and more conversation about deals. They would take Bellamy or Van Arsdale or Komives or Bryant or even Walt Frazier. We were interested in a few players around the league, ourselves. But whenever Eddie mentioned them, the conversation generally turned in other directions.

Detroit, for example, was looking for a center. What centers did we have? Bellamy and Bowman. The Pistons were interested in Bellamy. Then Eddie said, as he always

97

said when he talked to Detroit, we were only interested in Dave DeBusschere. I can tell you that the Knicks were interested in DeBusschere from the day he was drafted by the Pistons. They got him as a territorial choice in 1962 otherwise they might have had some competition.

Every time Donovan talked with Detroit through the years, he mentioned DeBusschere. Even when Dave was player-coach. We used to kid DeBusschere about trading himself to the Knicks. He was well aware of our efforts, since he was the coach and had access to information like that.

"I could help the Knicks," DeBusschere said not long after I took over the team. He had been replaced as coach by then and was only playing. The rumors about Bellamy had broken out again and it was around the deadline for trades. "They have trouble playing the two big men together," Dave added, meaning Reed and Bellamy. "If I had to leave, I would have liked to have come to New York, but Detroit is my home and I'm satisfied where I am."

That was in February 1968. You would have to say Mr. DeBusschere has a pretty good insight into the game of basketball. We were having trouble playing Bellamy and Reed together. They were both centers and kept getting in each other's way. Bells liked to play the middle and so did Willis. I played them together when I thought it would work and I split them when I thought that was best.

I knew we were on the road to somewhere when we finally beat the Celtics in a regular season game in Boston. Not only that, we spotted them twenty points and came on to win, 110–108. The Knicks had won a game in the 1967 playoffs up there, but otherwise they had lost tweny-five in a row dating back to December 22, 1962. So the victory, though nothing special in the standings, really made the players feel great.

Reed, Bellamy, Van Arsdale, Barnett, Komives and Bryant had suffered a lot at the hands of the Celtics in Boston. They remembered one game where they led by twenty-one with 8:45 to go but still lost. So beating the Celts on their floor was something extra. "Personally," said Frazier, who had just come into the league, "I never liked the Celtics." He didn't like them because they won so much. He had a lot of company in the NBA.

February 12, 1968, was a night to remember. We played our last game in the old Garden. We were moving from a $5,000,000 slum structure to a $120,000,000 complex. We closed it out with a big splash. We beat the 76ers and Chamberlain, 115–97. Frazier was just magnificent. He had fifteen rebounds, fifteen assists, twenty-three points and harassed Greer into only fifteen points for forty-one minutes.

"Maybe, I'll be remembered for what I did tonight," said Frazier, only three when the original Knicks began in the Garden in 1946. "That's the way to go," said Reed. "Play the champs, beat them badly and leave the building. Go out in proud style."

Barnett scored the last basket but did not appreciate the significance until someone asked if he wanted the basketball or should it be sent to the Hall of Fame. "I wasn't thinking about it, but, I'll tell you, make the shot dramatic as long as you're writing about it," he told reporters. Was there a bigger moment in his life? "Yeah," he smiled. "Payday."

Most Knicks were just too young to understand the nostalgia attached to the old Garden. It had a lot of memories for me. I played college ball there for Nat Holman at CCNY, where I got the best education any player or coach could get. I played pro ball there for the Rochester Royals. I scouted and coached for the Knicks in that building. I spent many years of my life there.

I guess the one thing that will stick in my mind forever was the night of the famous blackout of November 9, 1965. I remember we were supposed to play St. Louis. I got into the office early—around one in the afternoon. Selma had come to New York with me but had gone to the movies first. She was going to meet me later and see the game.

Selma got to my office around 5:30 or 6 o'clock. I was in Eddie Donovan's office and we were chatting when the lights went off. We didn't know what it was. We thought a fuse blew in the building. I guess everybody in the city must have thought the same thing at the same time. It's probably the first time in history that the people in New York ever were in precise agreement about anything.

We sat around waiting for the lights to go on, until we learned what had happened by listening to the radio. The players kept calling in. We finally told them the ball game was off. It was the first one in my memory ever called on account of darkness.

Selma and I waited until around eight o'clock watching the traffic jam on Eighth Avenue, and then decided to drive home. We had three passengers. One was Harriet Spaeth, a secretary. The others were Frank Ceragher, who ran the master clock and scoreboard, and Jimmy Wergeles of the publicity department. They all lived on Long Island, on our way home.

We piled into the car, and I drove. I cut across Fiftieth Street going east. I was heading for the Queensborough Bridge on Fifty-ninth Street. It was pitch black and the streets were jammed with cars and people. There was no power, so there were no subways or railroad trains. Either you used ground transportation or you checked into a hotel—if you were lucky enough to find a room.

We had the radio on all the time and got a bit of startling news. They said that everyone should shut off oil burners. When the power went on again, there was the possibility of an explosion if the oil burner was on. Selma and I really choked on that one.

How were we going to get to Cedarhurst when we couldn't even get downtown? We were lucky in one respect. Gail, our daughter, was away at Farleigh Dickinson, so we didn't have to worry about her. Now all we had to think about was possibly getting home and finding none. Instant ashes.

I groped my way downtown. "You know," said Harriet, "I think we're in a park." A park? Now what would a park be doing in the middle of the street? "I think it's a park," she insisted. "I see benches." She's nuts, I thought.

Well, what do you know? They are benches, aren't they? And I am driving through a park. Right smack through the middle of it on the pedestrian walk. I did the best I could under the circumstances. I went straight ahead. Somehow, I got out without taking a bench with me.

I didn't have the slightest idea where I was. I just kept going. I made another turn and what do you think happened? I was at the entrance to the bridge at the head of all the traffic. I was grinning like a genius. "You coach the same way," said Selma, who took the time out to say that before going back to worrying about our oil burner.

It was clear sailing once we got over the bridge and out of the city. I guess we got home about eleven o'clock. We were probably the only ones happy to see the blackout still on. Selma ran down to the basement to shut off the oil burner. I went upstairs to the bedroom.

I walked into a closet and instinctively yanked on the light string. The light went on. "Selma!" I screamed. "Look, there's a light in our closet." I figured we had the only light in the city. "The blackout's over, you dummy," said Selma. The darn thing, believe it or not, ended just as we stopped the furnace and I pulled the string in my closet.

O
10

Soon after I took over the Knicks from Dick McGuire, I had a conversation with Willis Reed about Walt Frazier. "Will, what about Frazier," I asked the captain. "Did I make a big mistake about him in my scouting report?"

I really didn't think so. I knew Frazier was an exceptional player but I liked to keep Reed involved. He was the team captain and he had his finger on the pulse of everything. "I don't think so," said Willis. "I just think he's got to be made to realize that he's better than he thinks he is. If he doesn't believe it, he's not going to think much of himself and he won't do much for me."

By the time we opened the new Garden against San Diego, there was no doubt that Frazier had made a believer of himself and everyone. Just to make sure, he stole the ball and scored our first basket in the new place. Do you know who got the first basket in the Garden? A young man named Dave DeBusschere of the Detroit Pistons. He hit it in the opening game of the doubleheader against the Boston Celtics. Symbolic?

We beat the Rockets that first night in the new Garden, 114–102, and Frazier had another good game. They were coming more often. The thing that impressed me was the way our players began picking him up. They looked to give him the ball. I never had to tell them that. It came naturally. They trusted him. They had faith in his ability, his leadership.

Frazier was not afraid of the responsibility. He wanted the ball when the pressure was on. I remember one night in Baltimore when it got him in trouble. We had what appeared to be a safe lead, if there is such a thing in pro ball. The Bullets needed three baskets to win and there were only a few seconds to go.

Baltimore scored and Frazier took the ball out. A steal and a basket. Walt took the ball out again. Another steal. This time there was a miss and then the buzzer finally sounded. We had won but when I reached the dressing room, Frazier was mad. He was ripping, to be exact.

I never saw him that disturbed. We listened. We allowed him to get it out of his system. "Okay, Walt, that's enough," I said when it looked as though he was running out of steam.

It was touchy but not unusual. Things like that happen, even to Frazier who is easygoing by nature. The best thing is to let the angry one blow it out, making sure his rage remains isolated and doesn't set off an explosion. He soon calmed down and we talked it over and no harm was done. Forgotten quicker than it started.

There always is biting here and there. Complaints about how the game was played or should be played. If two people can't live under the same roof without some arguments, how can twelve or thirteen? There was good rapport and we weren't even winning that much. That is what really counted.

When Frazier got mad, no one sulked or got angry with him. They realized he was motivated by what was good for the Knicks. He was trying to tell them to come to the

103

ball when the ball handler is stuck with it. They knew he was right. They would lose a lot of games if they kept making mistakes like that. They couldn't expect him to dribble the ball back onto the floor himself, although I saw that happen once or twice. Komives did it in one game and actually got away with it.

A lot of strange things happen if you see enough basketball games. Like another night in Baltimore. I keep asking myself how come so many things happen in Baltimore. Maybe it's Earl Monroe. This was a night when The Pearl got only forty points and wiped out a nice lead of fifteen that it had taken us so long to gain.

The game was tied at 116 and Monroe had created an emotional storm as usual. Van Arsdale went in for a layup and LeRoy Ellis jammed it. Johnson picked up the loose ball at the head of the key and fired to Monroe, breaking downcourt.

Earl tore for the basket from one side and Dick Barnett sped down the other side, trying to cut him off at the pass. Barnett got there. So did Monroe. There was a crunch of bodies. The ball went in. The place went wild. No one seemed to notice referee Jake O'Donnell waving that the basket was no good.

I noticed it. I also saw O'Donnell signaling a foul on Monroe for charging. I had to admire Jake. I have to admire NBA officiating in that respect. Not just because the call went our way. Monroe and all the excitement he had generated and the Baltimore crowd never entered Jake's mind. He called it exactly the way he felt it had happened, and so what if it was against the home team.

Jake soon found out "so what." There was stunned silence at first. And then anger. The natives moved nearer to the sidelines. O'Donnell was looking toward the scorer's table when something hit his leg. He turned. He looked around. He looked down. He was being attacked by a midget.

Earl Strom saved O'Donnell by calling the special cops and getting the little man thrown out. When order was restored, Monroe was out of the game with his sixth foul, and we went on to win, 126–122.

I can't help but think what might have happened in the Syracuse of the old days on a call like that. They were some fans. Rabid would be putting it mildly. There was one elderly woman who would sit in the front row at every game and rip the officials. She'd be on her feet, screaming whenever a call went against Syracuse. One night she even ran onto the floor to swing an umbrella.

Winning the night the new Garden opened put us at .500 once more and we began aiming at the playoffs. We were 32-32 with eighteen games to go and the race was very tight. Detroit was behind us with 29-34, then Cincinnati with 28-34 and Baltimore was last with 26-36. We didn't know it at the time, but we were to clinch third place on March 17 in San Francisco.

We were not a smooth machine, and we were still losing our share. But we were playing better team ball. It always helps when other people notice it. "I was with Billy Cunningham," said Richie Guerin, "and he told me he hoped the Knicks didn't finish third." That was a nice compliment. If we finished third, that meant we would be meeting the 76ers in the playoffs, if they kept going and finished first. So Billy was saying he preferred to play someone other than the Knicks.

Our players were flattered but words are only words. They still are no substitute for hard work and the fun of winning. "The personnel they always had," Guerin also said. "Now they really believe in themselves. They've finally become a team. They've gotten pride and they don't beat themselves. I don't write them off against anybody. They can beat anyone."

Richie was right. We had become a team. You could tell by little things, like the time Cazzie showed up when he wasn't supposed to and helped us beat Chicago and Detroit. He was doing his National Guard duty in Chicago and got finished around 5 P.M. and flew right to New York.

He arrived at the Garden about twenty minutes before the game with the Bulls and without his uniform. He had left it at the hotel because he did not expect to play. His spare was at the cleaner. We crayoned his Number Thirty-three on the back of a dummy shirt and he scored twenty-two. The next night in Detroit he hit thirty-eight.

His great desire to play was significant. He could have taken the easy way out and remained in Chicago. But he wanted to be part of everything the team was doing. Cazzie was like that. All the Knicks were like that. That was one reason why they had been so receptive to pulling together and working hard to accomplish something with meaning.

The newspapers made a big deal when we won our thirty-sixth game and equalled the previous season's total. They also pointed out we had a great shot at winning forty for the first time in ten years. It's funny how you get involved with things like that and lose your perspective. You become consumed by what you are doing and what is best for you; there is no time to think about anything but winning basketball games.

Donnie Butcher, for example, was in hot water in Detroit. His team was losing and his job was in jeopardy. Yet, the nature of the game was to beat the Pistons' brains out. There is no other way. Butcher knew that. He was well aware that if the situations were reversed, and another coach's job was on the line, he was obligated to bury the other team if possible.

106

All coaches go through it. So do players. You do your job and hope you can retain a sense of humor. Butcher not only lost to us but drew two technicals and was thrown out. I'll always remember what he said in the middle of all that frustration. "Everything is bad when you lose," he explained. "I've got a French poodle that's even barking at me now."

We went to Los Angeles needing a victory to clinch a playoff spot. We had used the zone press to win in Baltimore and Philadelphia and the confidence was there. We had the other teams worrying about it, and that was something. Jackson was playing seven feet tall. He has those long arms and he uses them like a windmill. And you know how hard it is to throw anything through a windmill when it is spinning.

We did not win in Los Angeles. We were bombed by Elgin Baylor. He was supposed to be getting old. He was supposed to be crippled. But he hit eleven of his first fourteen shots and scored thirty-seven points. We lost, 123–112. We had another bomb scare that night. It was funny when it was over.

Someone called the Forum switchboard around 9:45 and said there was a bomb planted in the building. We were using our zone press around that time to knock down a nineteen-point deficit to seven with five and a half minutes to go. We'll never know what would have happened if we had somehow gone in front. We do know that we were not advised about the situation until after the game. We were told to dress fast and get out of the building. We didn't need a bomb scare to prompt that. Baylor and West had accomplished it many times long before bomb scares became fashionable.

Game number eighty in San Francisco did it for us. We beat the Warriors, 130–104, and we were in the playoffs. We had won forty-one with two games to go. We wound up the season at 43-39. We had hit bottom at 15-25 when we dropped my first two games as coach and then went on to 28-14. We won five of our last seven and that made us feel good.

Philadelphia wound up first and we finished third, so we met in the playoffs. The opening game was in Convention Hall and Chamberlain was too much. We threw the zone press at the 76ers four different times. It kept us in it but we still lost, 118–110, because of Wilt.

He was devastating. He played forty-eight minutes in a game we accelerated as much as we could. He simply ground Bellamy and Reed into little pieces. He scored thirty-eight points and took down twenty-nine rebounds. "I'm strong but I couldn't hold him off," said Willis. "He was a wild man tonight, the way he went to the offensive board. He took me, Walt and everyone with him."

We tied it in the Garden. Chamberlain played forty-eight minutes and got only seventeen rebounds. "The Knicks were more aggressive," was Wilt's explanation after we won, 128–117. I don't know. We were just as aggressive in Philadelphia but we lost. We always play to keep Wilt from getting the ball in deep where he wants it. Sometimes you do, sometimes you don't.

Wilt is great but there are times when he can't control the game the way everyone seems to expect from him. He has been so super, he always gets blamed when his team loses. It's not that simple. There are five players on that floor trying to bother and stop him. When they do, his team can lose. When they don't, his team can win. But there are no guarantees because it is a team game and always will be.

It's like expecting Mickey Mantle to win every game with a homer. People forget there is a pitcher out there who is being paid to stop him. It is no secret that the teams overload their defenses to force Wilt to give up the ball or go away from the board. I would say he suffered so much abuse mainly because he has such great talent. People could never understand how come he did not beat Bill Russell more often. It is possible that the Boston Celtics simply had the better team. One man can be the difference but he never is the whole team. Not even Russell. Not even Chamberlain.

We beat Wilt and the 76ers twice in the 1968 playoffs. They beat us four times. We managed to escape with our first victory. We were leading 71–53 at one time and Philadelphia came back to 96–93 with nine minutes to play. There was no way I could sit still and watch it all go. There is no way you can coach scared basketball, either.

Jackson, for example, had a rough time in the opener. It was his first playoff game and he was shaky. But that was another night. Phil was an important part of the team. The situation called for him and in he went. I wanted to give Reed a blow. I wanted to nurse as much of the lead as I could while Willis was on the bench.

"It took a lot of guts," said one reporter. Nonsense. If a guy doesn't coach like that, he doesn't belong. Jackson went in and scored six big points. He only got eight altogether. He left with two minutes to go but we had the game by then.

Jackson has a great knack for getting in the way of the other team. Billy Cunningham found that out in the third game. It was a wild one played in the Palestra and we lost in double overtime. Philadelphia, however, had worse trouble. Cunningham collided with Jackson and was lost to the 76ers for the rest of the playoffs with a broken wrist. To this day, Wilt insists that is why Boston eliminated Philadelphia in the Eastern final after our series. Who can say he is wrong?

We looked like we had this one all the way. With six

seconds to go in regulation, Chet Walker tied the score and sent it into overtime. Then we had the ball in front court with a three-point lead and only nineteen seconds remaining in the first overtime when they tied it again. Impossible? We were killing the clock when the ball was deflected backcourt by Matt Guokas and picked up by Hal Greer for a basket.

Cazzie took the ball out. He passed and Greer banged it loose, then missed a driving layup. But Guokas, trailing the play, got the rebound and was fouled while shooting. He made one of two to send it into the second overtime at 125 and the 76ers went on to win, 138–132. It was a whacky game. Earl Strom, one of the refs, even got into an argument with a belligerent fan in the front row and they wound up kicking each other.

We took the fourth game at home, 107–98, but Johnny Green, of all people, ruined us in the next one down in Philly. He had been obtained by the 76ers from San Diego a few weeks earlier for about twenty thousand dollars and a third-draft choice. Jack Ramsay, the general manager and coach, wanted him as insurance at forward.

Green was just that. He stepped in when Cunningham broke his wrist, shot 7-for-12 and grabbed eleven rebounds in a game we could have won. We lost, 123–105, and the 76ers had a 3-2 lead. We went to Philadelphia without Frazier, who popped a tendon in his calf early in the second period. He was through for the playoffs no matter what.

We were finished when the 76ers came to the Garden and won the final game, 113–97. We had lost but we had done very well. It might have been different if we had won that third game in Philadelphia. It might have been different if Frazier had not gotten hurt and missed the last two games. "They will be right up there next year, fighting with us," said Chamberlain.

110

O

11

"I can't wait to see if we are as great as everyone says we are," said Dick Barnett as the 1968-69 season was about to open. There had been a few changes in the NBA but everyone seemed to be excited about the Knicks. I guess it was the way we closed out the 1967-68 season.

It had to be that. On the face of it, we did not figure to be any stronger at the beginning. We had just lost Dick Van Arsdale, Emmette Bryant and Neil Johnson in the expansion draft. How could you lose players like that and be better?

Only one team was hit harder, I guess. Philadephia had lost Chamberlain. He insisted on being traded when the 76ers could not come to a financial agreement with him. So Wilt went to the Lakers for Darrall Imhoff, Archie Clark, and Jerry Chambers who had gone into the army for two years.

It had to be a tough decision for Jack Ramsay and owner Irv Kosloff. There was bound to be some effect on the 76ers without Chamberlain. We also had a tough decision to make. We had to put Van Arsdale in the expansion pool and that really hurt. It hurt us and it hurt Van.

Everyone seemed to feel that Barnett had to go because he was getting old. That made Eddie Donovan and me laugh. Barnett was irreplaceable in our situation. He was an outstanding team player. He was smart. If we let him go, who would take his place? Bradley had not yet shown he could do the job consistently in the backcourt. Komives and Bryant were small guards. We needed Barnett's size and shooting and knowledge.

Donovan and I tried to think of some scheme to keep Van Arsdale. He was a great defensive player, and we were sold on defense. But he had to go into the pool. We could only protect seven. We picked Donnie May three days later in the regular draft because he was a Van Arsdale-type forward. We also had chosen Bill Hosket in the first-round draft that had been staged earlier so as not to give the ABA too big a jump on the college players.

May and Hosket were no Van Arsdales. They were two good ballplayers who had started out together as high school teammates in Dayton and now were on the same pro team. Hosket had been away with the Olympic team, but May reported to training camp at the State University of New York in Farmingdale, Long Island. So did Mike Riordan—again.

Mike had played well in the Eastern league and deserved another look. He was in our camp for the second time but really was a rookie. He was not familiar with our routine but soon found out it was work. Riordan was lucky in that respect. He liked work. He liked practice. Others couldn't stand it, but they worked hard because it was their job and their obligation.

There were no big projects. We just picked up where we left off at the end of the previous season. We worked mostly on defense, as usual. The offense got some attention. We rolled along nicely except for the preseason game we lost to the Olympic team. For us, it was a workout. For them, it was a crusade.

Spencer Haywood, then only nineteen, was something. He scored, rebounded and even blocked some of our shots. Hosket, our man, also played for the Olympic team. Reed, always the diplomat, struck a blow for patriotism. "I'm glad they won," he said after the Knicks lost, 65–64, in overtime.

The training camp helped Bradley the most. It was his first with us. You could see the difference. He was relaxed and comfortable. He was in the flow of things. He was doing things naturally. We had talked of the pressure of pro basketball. I suggested that he just take his time—it would come.

"I know what he's going through," Russell said. "I know what I went through. I used to be tight just thinking about defense. The kid has started off with the players this year. You can see his timing is back. His quick step is back. Don't take the kid lightly."

Bradley, the kid, was a year older than he but that made no difference to Cazzie. My purpose was to use the preseason games to sharpen our defense. We had no major problems about giving new players time. We only had two that mattered—May and Riordan whose size and gung-ho attitude had earned him a spot.

We opened the season in the Garden against Chicago amid rave notices. "I'm not even considering what happened last season," Jack Ramsay had said. "I'm going on just what I've seen. It looks to me like New York is the toughest." Another guy suggested the Knicks were wasting their time playing the season—they should head straight for the Hall of Fame.

Richie Guerin of Atlanta was a first-nighter and he kidded me and Donovan about winning the whole thing by ten games. There was an opening-night band in the house. All the trimmings of something big except for one thing—the Knicks lost. The Bulls beat us, 100–96.

They had a new coach, Dick Motta, and Jerry Sloan and Flynn Robinson had to play almost the entire game in the backcourt because of injuries. But they beat us in our first game. Was Motta overwhelmed? Well. . . . "That was a big one for me," he confessed. "But I've had bigger ones. I once won the championship in high school of the whole state of Idaho."

I guess Cazzie said it best. "The answer is we can't go out and talk a good year," he explained. "Last year is gone. The only thing people remember about last year is that Boston beat Philadelphia. They don't even remember that Boston beat Los Angeles."

We lost the next game. It was to the Lakers at home. With Chamberlain, of course. We were just bad. Reed got only three baskets on fifteen shots and wound up with seven points for thirty-one minutes. I wasn't satisfied with a thing.

Back to practice. Our timing was off. We were not playing together. It was there. We just had to do it. "It's early, there are eighty more games to play," said Elgin Baylor. I was glad he reminded us.

We finally made it in our third game. We beat the 76ers in the Garden but it took some great clutch shooting by Cazzie. He hit three quick baskets under the gun and we won, 117–114. A lot of guys don't want the ball in a spot like that. Cazzie wants it. I don't mind going down the drain with a guy like that shooting the ball.

What I didn't like was the way Philly zone-pressed us. Ramsay is a smart coach. He knows all the tricks. But I thought we could handle the press better. One reason why I put it in was so that we could learn how to handle it. I believe in that. If a team hurts us with something,

114

I'm not afraid to borrow it. We not only learn how to use it but we also learn how to beat it.

We let Philly come from 109–94 back to tie at 110. The zone press can do that if you don't know how to attack it. You must keep shooting. You cannot go into a freeze. The more you handle the ball, the more likely someone will steal. You got to keep attacking.

It was not our only problem. Things went so badly, I had to make some moves after we blew an eighteen-point lead and lost in Detroit. The next night, in Seattle, I decided to let Frazier come off the bench and start Komives and Barnett in the backcourt. Then I started Komives and Bradley and let Barnett come off the bench.

We were eleven games into the season and had won only five. "John Havlicek, Jr.," was Frazier's reaction to his not starting. "That's what I was doing last year. It helped me to come off the bench then. Because I was a rookie, it took the pressure off me. I'm ready to do any-thing—anything to win."

We saw Elvin Hayes for the first time in San Diego and lost. We went to San Francisco and lost on a bank shot by Jeff Mullins with three seconds to go. We went to Los Angeles and lost on two fouls by Jerry West with seven seconds left.

Things were going really badly. We were getting testy. Donovan came out to see what was going on. I could only think of the Dick McGuire situation a year ago. This time, it was Eddie who was sick, not the coach. I'm just not a worrier. I like to lose less than the next guy, but when the game is over, win or lose, it's scotch and steak and to bed. People get so uptight after the damage is done. For what? Why add to the aggravation? One time in our house, Selma was having the den redone. They ripped the whole room apart. It was some mess.

While they were working, the ceiling collapsed. It was their problem and we didn't worry about that. They went home and that night, we thought the house was a little warmer than usual. It was winter, so we figured the workmen had turned up the thermostat to get more heat.

It really got hot. We couldn't stand it. Selma went downstairs to look around. I heard her yell. I ran down. She was standing at the top of the basement stairs. "Look," she said, pointing to the basement. I looked. The place was flooded. The water almost was up to the third step. Selma was ready to cry. I wasn't too happy. But what I was going to do?

The damage was done. I said the first thing that came to mind. "Selma," I said. "Who'd ever think that a poor boy like me from Brooklyn would ever have a swimming pool in his basement?" She broke up. We sat on the top step and laughed. It cost money to have the boiler fixed. Would it have cost less if we had gotten upset and screamed at the water in the basement?

I had my share of anxious moments, of course. I had one in the Los Angeles game. Wilt and Willis got in a mixup. Chamberlain was in close for a stuff shot and Reed pinned his arms. There was some shoving and some words. "You got to protect yourself at all times," said Wilt, explaining why he reacted with a push. "It was a legitimate play," insisted Willis, who had pushed back. They agreed someone could get hurt over a silly spat like that and Willis suggested it could be both of them.

Donovan chatted with Bob Feerick of San Francisco and Freddie Schaus of Los Angeles but had no deals in mind. We were satisfied with our personnel and decided to keep going with what we had. It had to change. The players were getting the hang of helping each other on defense. We lost again in Los Angeles and wound up the trip with a 1-5 record.

I guess everyone was disappointed, especially Hosket. He had returned from the Olympics and joined us in the Garden for our ninth game. He had expected better as had everyone else. We lost his first game to Baltimore and he came along with us on the Coast trip that saw us drop and drop.

I started Bowman over Reed against Cincinnati when we returned to the Garden and we lost our fifth straight. We were six games under .500. We were five and eleven. Milwaukee, the new team in our division had dropped only eight games. Not good at all.

"Too bad Red didn't save some of the way they played last year and bottle it," suggested Jack McMahon of San Diego. Again rumors that we were going to deal Bellamy. Again stories that Barnett finally was starting to play old at thirty-two. Again innuendos that we had made a terrible mistake by keeping Dick and letting Van Arsdale go in expansion.

We did miss Van Arsdale at that stage. He would have been a stabilizing influence. But he was gone. We had made that decision and it was based on the fact that we had the players to compensate for his loss. The team just was not playing together. There was a little something missing.

We lost in Atlanta and fell seven games under .500. The next day in Boston, I called off practice and held a meeting. We had lost ten of our last twelve games and it was my job to get the team out of it. I talked to players about a few things that were going wrong. I discussed what they should be doing.

We won that night in Boston. We beat the Chicago Bulls, 114–107, after being down, 87–78. We had some serious problems when we were losing by nine because Cazzie and Bradley were in foul trouble. They each had five personals. I put Barnett at forward and had Frazier pick up Barry Clemens at the other end. A little later, I sent in Hosket and he got six points and six rebounds in seven minutes. Everything worked. The tension seemed to break. Our dressing room was wild. The players congratulated each other. It looked like we had just won a championship.

"Victory party in the Commodore," shouted Whelan. "Starts at midnight. Guy Lombardo will be there. No turtlenecks." Whelan was just great. No team ever had a better trainer. No coach ever had a guy like him who did as much to create a togetherness. He could be tough with the players or make them laugh. They loved him.

Everyone was surprised about Barnett playing forward. So was Dick. "That's the first time I've done that since I was with Syracuse," he pointed out. "I have an advantage. I'm small and quick." Then there was Hosket. He had gone into the game in some spot. From his viewpoint, not mine.

Hosket was on the team, so he was capable of playing in any game at any time. The fact that we were in danger of losing never entered my mind. We needed a big forward and Hos was it. Reed, nevertheless, made a big deal of it, especially since Hos had hit his first shot.

"That took a lot of guts," Willis said to Hosket. "That's what happens when you're my roommate." Hosket gave Willis one of his big, boyish grins. These two were to become good friends. I'd always get a kick out of seeing them walking through airports and Willis, with an arm around Hosket's shoulder, talking to him like a big brother.

That is why Reed was made captain. He is a born leader. He knows how to talk to people. They respect him. I never saw a guy with his nature. It's remarkable. I should know. I put it to him plenty when we first started. I screamed at him more than anyone. Not because he was making more mistakes, but he helped get the message across.

I really broke his chops at the beginning. I would yell at him about getting back on defense and turning his head and picking up a man. He'd run by the bench sometimes and plead his case. I would accuse him of trying to sneak a rest. He was just great. I never could have gotten away with it if he wasn't such a sweet guy.

Oh, he'd get mad. He wouldn't be human if he took all my abuse without snapping back. But the minute the game ended, or the minute the practice ended, it was all forgotten. Willis is just a big, good-natured guy. He'll do just about anything for anybody. A great player and a great person.

That is why I always room a rookie with him. Hosket was a good example. Something rubbed off on him. Maybe it was confidence. Willis has a way of making people feel comfortable. Hosket helped us win that game in Boston and things got better rather fast.

As I look back, I'd have to say that little talk we had in Boston represented one major crisis in the lives of the Knicks. We played the Celtics next in the Garden and we were not yet accustomed to beating them. But we won, 111–100, and Bellamy did a fine job against Russell. Not many centers ever got eleven rebounds and thirteen points in the first quarter on Russell. The big Bells wound up with twenty-four rebounds and twenty-nine points.

"Bellamy can play like that," said Sam Jones. "If he comes to play like that, the record could be reversed. He's got to play ball. He'll get up for Russ and Chamberlain and Thurmond but he should also get up for Finkel." Everyone was puzzled by Bellamy. He had the equipment to be a supercenter.

Bellamy and I talked many times. No matter what he did, you always felt he could do more. The players felt that way. So did the fans. Maybe everyone expected too much from him. It was not easy to determine what Bellamy felt. He said very little. He was asked what he thought about the booing he got before his big performance against Russell. "I guess they want me to play better," he replied softly.

Everyone played better from then on. Three nights later we made it three in a row by beating Chamberlain and the Lakers for the first time. This time it was Bradley. We were losing, 91–81, with four minutes to go. I sent Bradley and Frazier in to help Jackson with the zone press. Everything went right.

Jackson hit two quick baskets and Bradley got three more out of the press. We won, 104–100, and once more the dressing room scene was something. "Dollar Bill! Dollar Bill!" shrieked Cazzie. "Superman!" yelled Komives. They were all happy for Bradley. They knew what he had been going through.

Butch van Breda Kolff, then coaching the Lakers, made a pertinent observation about the Garden fans. The crowd of 15,024 had been the largest since Bradley's first game. It indicated the interest and excitement that could be generated by a winning Knick team. It told Butch something else.

"There were fifteen thousand in there and only a dozen of us," he said. He seemed to be saying that the noise and our press had something to do with his team throwing the ball away so much. Could be.

I later discovered how true it was—how important the New York fans could be with their vocal support. How much their enthusiasm would inspire the Knicks and put pressure on the other team. It had been so long since the Knicks had a winning team, we had forgotten such things were possible.

We kept winning. Atlanta came into the Garden for our

first meeting with the Hawks since some of the players had a scuffle. Guerin remarked, "We have signed Joe Frazier and Sonny Liston for the rematch and we are working out at Stillman's gym."

The game was not that funny. We won, 126–93, and Guerin was upset. His players heard about it at half time. Richie was so mad, he even put himself in the game in the first quarter. He had reinstated himself although he was out of shape because there were injuries in the backcourt. But no one ever questioned Guerin's courage.

Guerin, playing, did not help. Guerin, coaching, did not help. It was one of those games. "They picked us up right away and put the pressure on us and their full-court press threw us off," explained Bill Bridges. "They hadn't stopped us for the last five years—since I've been a Hawk." He treated it like an accident. It wasn't.

We were moving. I knew it. The players knew it. You could tell the way we were winning and enjoying it. We were loose. We were playing together. We were helping out. All those hours of hard work in training camp and in practices finally were beginning to pay off.

We lost Bellamy for the final fourteen minutes of the Atlanta game but Reed, with help from Bowman, did the job at center very well. The team was learning how good it was. So was the coach. I had a very flexible squad at my disposal. There were a lot of things I could do in an emergency.

Reed, for instance. I knew what he could do at center if something happened to Bellamy. I knew we wouldn't be in trouble. The defense was better with Willis at center because he was more active. But as long as Bellamy was on the team, he had to play. He had too much ability to keep him on the bench.

O

12

The phone rang in my room in Boston. It was Eddie Donovan. We were in constant touch whenever the Knicks were on the road. He always wanted to know what went on in the ball games and how the guys were playing and things like that.

That's what made Eddie an excellent general manager. He was on top of everything all the time. This time he wanted to talk about the discussions he was having with other teams. We had straightened out and finally reached .500 by beating San Francisco at home. We now were on a two-game road trip: Boston and then Detroit.

It was rather unusual for him to call so soon after we had left home but there was a good reason. Detroit was very interested in Bellamy. He had been talking to the Pistons for about two weeks. He had been talking to other teams, but the conversation with Detroit had heated up.

"I think it's time to go after DeBusschere again," Eddie said. He felt his discussions with Ed Coil, general manager of the Pistons, had reached that point. Detroit needed a center badly and Paul Seymour, who had replaced Donnie Butcher as coach, was interested in Bellamy.

Seymour had Bellamy in Baltimore and knew him well. Paul was desperate for a big man and it seemed to Detroit that Bellamy was the best one available. The Pistons had analyzed our situation and figured we were moving along slowing with no staggering progress in victories. They felt we had Reed to play center and Bowman for backup, so Bellamy might be expendable.

That is why the trade discussion with Detroit got more intense than the others. The Pistons made it obvious they wanted Bellamy badly. We wanted only one man, but Eddie carefully avoided mentioning DeBusschere in the preliminary stages because he didn't want to get turned down again. There could be only one deal for Bellamy as far as we were concerned. It had to be DeBusschere or nothing.

"We'll probably have to give more for DeBusschere than Bellamy," Donovan said, "but it's worth trying. Let's see what they have to say." Eddie had it figured perfectly. He had been through it before. He had been on the other side so many times. He had been the one looking for help.

Deals are the same for everyone. You must make up your mind that the player you want is going to help and then determine what to give. It had been said a thousand times but it is worth repeating—when you make a trade, you think of only helping your team and cannot worry about the players you give up.

That was what Detroit had in mind by attempting to solve its biggest problem at center. And that's what we had in mind by attempting to get DeBusschere. As far as we were concerned, Dave was the only one on Detroit who could help our situation and was worth giving up Bellamy. So Eddie went back to the phone and I went to the Boston Garden for a game with the Celtics.

We won that night and climbed over .500, finally. On November 21 we were 6-13 and on December 18, we went to 18-17 by beating Boston in Boston, 104–98. Reed and Barnett had big scoring games. Frazier and Jackson toughened our defense. Bellamy helped by giving Russell a tough time. Bells shot only 4-for-15 but played forty-eight minutes and drove enough to go to the line fourteen times and make ten.

There was no one man responsible for the win and that was good. If we were going to be a team, a real team, everyone had to help. The players knew it and the scene in the dressing room was a happy one. They were coming more often. Beating Boston in Boston was always something special. Too many of the players had lived through all those games where the Celtics had beaten their brains out.

Butch Komives asked for permission to go directly to Toledo instead of staying with the team in Detroit. His mother was seriously ill. Ordinarily, the players live together on the road. No exceptions. This was something different. Butch left and we stayed at the Metropolitan Hotel in the Detroit Airport. It was far from town but it was convenient. We didn't have to get up early in the morning and fight traffic to make a plane. We try to stay near airports whenever we can find first-class accommodations.

The flight from Boston to Detroit was nothing unusual. I never even thought of the trade talk with the Pistons. We had been there so often. I knew that every time we mentioned DeBusschere, the talks stopped. It was no different with us. Whenever they mentioned Reed or Frazier, that was it. Donovan was not interested.

Atlanta, for example, had put out a feeler about Frazier when the Lennie Wilkens situation came to a head before the season started. Wilkens had become unhappy about his contract and a few other matters. He did not like the idea, he said, that the Hawks had invited Bill Bridges and

Gene Tormohlen on a State Department tour of Europe and had ignored him.

Richie Guerin stepped in where coaches generally fear to tread. No coach likes to get involved with the money matters of the players. It puts him in a position where it is hard to convince the players he is objective. A coach can only complicate his job if he enters salary negotiations. He can recommend one way or another if management asks for his opinion, but the best thing for all concerned is to let the front office handle the money.

Now don't ask me how that philosophy applies when the coach also is the general manager. As, for instance, Red Holzman. It can be sticky. But not as much in Madison Square Garden as out of town. The Garden has an organization that is available to help a general manager-coach in policies dealing with publicity, promotion, ticket sales and even salary negotiations. In other cities, one person has to handle that if he is general manager-coach and it can be tough.

Guerin was taking a calculated risk when he met with Wilkens to discuss the financial stalemate. They seemed to settle things. At least Richie thought so when the conference ended. The next thing that happened was Lennie said he still was not satisfied. He indicated he preferred not to play any longer for Atlanta.

That is when we, or Donovan, heard from the Hawks. There was no hard talk, only routine discussion. Somewhere along the way, the Hawks wanted to know if the Knicks would be interested in Wilkens. Who wouldn't? Donovan wanted to know for what or for whom? Frazier, maybe, it was suggested. Donovan cut off the conversation right there. Wilkens eventually went to Seattle where he got a good bounce and became player-coach.

We had no intention of trading Clyde, as Frazier was to be called by trainer Danny Whelan, who borrowed the nickname from the Bonnie and Clyde movie of the same name. It is true that Wilkens was an established backcourt star in the league and would be a great asset to any team. It was also true that Frazier still was having his problems and who could really tell if he would ever develop into a player as good as Wilkens?

But those are the decisions you have to make every now and then. We figured Clyde was younger, bigger and stronger and had the potential to be even better than Wilkens, if that was possible. We had no guarantees we were right. Our track record had indicated we had been wrong before at times. But we were sure we were right about Frazier.

Detroit found itself in the same position when Donovan went back to Coil and Seymour and threw DeBusschere's name at them. Coil had been over that track many times through the years and had always said no. Seymour was going through it for the first time and had a fresher viewpoint. He was the coach and he felt he had to be more objective. He could not be influenced by DeBusschere's being a local hero who had played high school, college and pro basketball in Detroit. He had a team that was in trouble and needed a center. He had had Bellamy before and he felt that was the answer.

Seymour was on an extension when Donovan got back to Coil and renewed their phone conversations. We were flying from Boston to Detroit when the talks resumed. I had no idea that we would wind up getting DeBusschere. Neither did Donovan. But he tried. For the first time, he did not get an outright rejection. The opening finally was there. Donovan walked through it.

It was provided when Seymour suggested that the Pistons could not swap DeBusschere even up for Bellamy. That was the first legitimate indication that the Pistons would even entertain the idea of trading Dave. That, in

126

itself, was a tribute to the perseverance and time Donovan had invested through the years. He wasn't about to
blow it. Not after getting that close. If the Pistons had to
have another player with Bellamy, that was fine, depend-
ing on what other player.

"Komives," Seymour suggested. Donovan had to think
about that. If we traded Komives, we would be down to
Barnett and Frazier as working guards. Bradley was
doubling up but appeared to be strongest at forward.
Riordan was being used to give fouls. Cazzie had long
since proved he was a forward. The departure of Komives would deplete the backcourt.

But, let's not kid ourselves. In all due respect to Komives and what he was capable of doing, and considering
the risk we might be taking with the backcourt, you just
don't turn down a DeBusschere. We had forwards but not
like him. There were very few forwards in the game who
were like him.

I guess it was around five in the afternoon on December 19, 1968, that the phone rang in my room at the
Metropolitan Hotel in the Detroit airport. It was Donovan.
I was in the room with a newspaperman and chased him
out when Eddie told me what had happened. "We got a
deal," Donovan said when I informed him the coast was
clear. "They'll take Bellamy, but they insisted on Komives
and I said it was a deal." Eddie and I agreed if we had to
give up Komives we would do it.

Donovan said both sides had to clear the deal with
management but the announcement should be made immediately, anyway. There was no way it could keep overnight, especially when all the players were in town and
we were playing a game the next night. I told Frankie
Blauschild, our publicity man, to alert the newspapermen
not to leave the hotel.

My job now was to inform Bellamy and Komives. I

started with Komives. I couldn't find him. I tried for hours. I finally reached his sister and gave her the message. I apologized for not telling Butch directly, but he had left to go home to see his mother and now was totally unavailable.

I told his sister because I figured that way, at least, he might get the news before he read a paper or heard it on the radio. That was beyond my control. Bellamy was another matter. He was in his room in the hotel. I went to see him. He was in bed watching television, I think. "Walter," I said. "There's been a deal made. We have traded you to Detroit." I told him about Komives and then I told him how sorry I was it had to be that way.

He looked at me. He never got out of bed. "That's the way it is," he said. No fuss. No anger. No long explanations. As simple as that. I walked out of his room a little relieved. I thought it would be tougher. I know it is always rough when you have to tell a player he is cut in training camp or is being traded.

Walter was great about it. It was possible he would have preferred to remain in New York. With Bellamy you never knew. He never mentioned a word. Maybe he was happy to be going where he would be the number one center again. I know this: I never heard Bellamy cry about anything that ever happened to him. He had his feelings and his viewpoint. But he never complained. He didn't when I told him he would be switching uniforms the next night with Komives.

I went to my room and got on the phone. I called DeBusschere at home. He had heard. The Pistons had called. I told him how happy we were about making the deal. He said how happy he was to be able to play in New York. I told him we'd get together before the game and we would talk things over.

I can say this now. I couldn't say it then. We knew

what we were getting in DeBusschere. He was a real pro. A fine team player. He could rebound and play defense. What we didn't know was what a great rebounder he really was for a guy his size. He could rebound with the biggest and the best. He fit perfectly and quickly into the very things we wanted to do.

He did it right away, in the first game the next night in Detroit. It was a strange thing for him to walk into the visiting clubhouse to dress. He got some greeting. He shook hands all around. You got the feeling that the players sensed this was something exceptional that had just happened to them.

DeBusschere explained how he got the news over the phone while trying to quiet his pet dog. Bellamy was in the other dressing room explaining how he was not the least bit surprised. "Anytime there was a trade possibility, I guess I was the prominent one," Bells said. "There's not any day of the season you can't expect anything to happen. The only thing you can do is relax and get something to eat."

He stole my philosophy, the big stiff. Komives dropped by our dressing room to pick up his stuff. I explained how I had tried to reach him. He said he understood. I know he felt badly about leaving New York. He had said so many times after his blow-up the season before. He had gotten to like New York and had planted his business roots there.

The departure of Komives and Bellamy had an immediate influence on some of our players. That is why I went to a few other rooms after the deal was made. I went to see Willis and told him he was going back to center. I went to see Bowman and told him he was the backup man for Reed. I went to Riordan's room and told him he would get more action with Komives gone. Now I know how those poor room-service guys must feel.

DeBusschere had some first game for us. We won, 135–87, and it was the widest margin of victory in the Knicks' twenty-two-year-history. DeBusschere was nervous and unbelievable. He played thirty-seven minutes and hit nine of his fifteen shots and pulled down a game-high fifteen rebounds and was just sensational.

He created a fever the minute he walked onto the floor. The fans, his old Detroit fans, gave him a fantastic greeting. He set them off again with seven rebounds in the first period and they rooted for him all night as though he had never changed uniforms.

You might say he had a slight inspirational effect on everyone. Bowman played twenty-four minutes, a minute more than Willis, and hit nine of his twelve shots. I must confess that was one fringe benefit of the deal we never expected that soon. Not that kind of shooting from Nate. We shot 59-for-109 but the best aspect was the defense. We limited the Pistons to eighty-seven shots and eighty-seven points and DeBusschere was a great help.

Dave confessed he had gotten a little tired. Emotion and lack of sleep. "I had only four hours sleep," he revealed. "Everyone was calling up at seven in the morning." I liked the way the players reacted to DeBusschere. "He's tough. So far so good," said Reed. "He gives us more movement," said Frazier. "I'll try like hell to make New York a winner," DeBusschere promised them.

There seemed to be some doubt that DeBusschere would make that much difference. Some people felt we made a mistake trading Bellamy. Some thought we would pay the price for stripping our backcourt by letting Komives go. "How are they going to make up Bellamy's statistics?" they said. "They used to hurt us with their size, now they don't," said Jack Ramsay of the 76ers.

We were in no position to afford the luxury of such guessing games. DeBusschere would be playing his next game in front of the Garden fans for the first time as a Knick. It was two nights after we won by forty-eight in Detroit. This time we beat Seattle by twenty-six. DeBusschere got a tremendous welcome.

New York fans know their basketball. Most of them grew up playing one-on-one and two-on-two in the school-yard. They recognized right away what DeBusschere meant to the team. They knew right away how much more efficient Reed would be at center. Those who didn't, found out rather quickly. We won eight straight with DeBusschere until the Chicago Bulls ended the streak.

We were running better, defending better, hitting the boards better and laughing better. I never felt you needed a superstar to win if you had five good players and a bench. Yes, it is nice to have a Bill Russell or Wilt Chamberlain or Oscar Robertson or Jerry West or Lew Alcindor, but not necessary. Some people say Willis Reed is a superstar. Some don't. To me he is.

What's in a label, anyway? Reed does the job for the Knicks and that is all that matters. He is a highly valuable individual. There were no most valuable players on the team. Frazier was as important as Reed, DeBusschere was as important as Frazier, Riordan was as important as Barnett and so on down the bench. It can't be any other way if the players want to be a team and win.

We found that out just before the all-star game. We left on a trip that was to take us to Chicago, Milwaukee, Phoenix, Oakland and San Diego. It started off with the end of our winning streak in Chicago Stadium. We had won two in a row before DeBusschere joined us and ran it to ten when the Bulls beat us, 102–101. Big Tom Boer-winkle hit a desperation hook halfway to the corner with fourteen seconds to go and Bob Weiss put it away with two fouls with four seconds remaining.

We were playing better team ball and, wherever we

went, they kept saying it was DeBusschere. He turned out to be the missing link, for sure. But don't ever forget that there were a lot of Knicks playing good ball before him and they played good ball after he joined the team.

I may be accused of talking like a coach and trying to butter up the players. But it's the truth. We had fine ball-players all along. They didn't need DeBusschere to prove that. What he did was help make the Knicks a better team. Who can tell how much? So many little things enter into it and we soon were given the opportunity to understand it better.

We won in Milwaukee, 115–101, and you could see the team loosening up. The ball handling was dazzling. They began zipping passes around with such speed and finesse, it brought back the good old days at City College under Nat Holman. How Red Phillips and I used to work the give-and-go on the other teams! And how they worked it on Red Phillips and me!

There was one play in Milwaukee that was a beauty. As Drew Pearson used to say: "It was a prediction of things to come." It was a fast break. Barnett flipped behind his back on the dead run to Frazier. Then Clyde did the same thing up ahead to Cazzie. The ball never touched the floor from midcourt and Caz laid it in.

Cazzie remained hot in Phoenix. He hit nine of his first ten shots and wound up with 13-for-17 and twenty-nine points. We won, 134–120. He left us there to go back to Chicago for reserve duty. We thought nothing of it. We were rolling. We were playing great basketball. Frazier was stealing his way through the West. In one spurt, he swiped the ball four times against the Suns.

We moved into Oakland and beat San Francisco. Our defense was just out of this world. We won, 85–77. Imagine, in this day and age of run and shoot, holding a pro basketball team to seventy-seven points. But it wasn't all peaches and sour cream. Phil Jackson had to leave the game just before the half. His back bothered him.

Phil couldn't remember when he had hurt himself. He said he first felt a little uncomfortable two weeks ago and thought it was the beds at home. We decided to see what happened overnight. Jackson could hardly walk the next day. We sent him to a doctor in San Diego and it was diagnosed as a slipped disc.

Frazier also reported in sick. He had the flu. He said he felt too weak to play against the Rockets that night but would go to the game and see. When we got to the dressing room, Clyde said he couldn't make it. Poor Jackson was standing over on the side of the room all crippled up in agony. I told Danny Whelan to get Jackson and Frazier out on the first plane.

There we were, without Frazier, Jackson and Cazzie. Not only that, Bradley said he didn't feel well. He was sick to his stomach and thought he had the flu. He said he could play, though. He had to sit on the bench in any event because with him we were down to the league minimum of eight players in uniform on the bench.

The guy came in for our starting lineup as is the custom. I told him Bradley and DeBusschere at the forwards, Reed at center, Barnett and Riordan at the guards. I was giving Mike his first start. I had Bowman, May and Hosket on the bench. If anything happened to them, it would have to be Whelan and me, in that order.

We somehow managed to get through the warm-up without any new developments. The game was ready to begin. Reed and Elvin Hayes were set for the tap. The ball was about to be tossed. Everyone was poised. Suddenly, Bradley turned and ran towards our bench. He never made it.

He stopped at the press table, alongside our bench, and threw up. Poor Danny Whelan. He had to wipe it off the floorboards with a towel. All I had to do was put someone in for Bradley. I chose May. He started his first game for a starter who didn't start.

I told Bradley to sit near me. He sat with a towel over his mouth and watched the game. "How do you feel?" I asked after a few minutes. "I'm ready," he said. I hadn't asked him that but I couldn't turn him down. In he went. He played for a while and then ran off the court to throw up again. Three times that happened but he wouldn't give in. What guts. What a mess for Whelan.

Bradley played thirty-seven minutes that night and had eleven assists and nine rebounds. We won, 105–102, as Reed hit thirty-six and DeBusschere twenty-six. But I'll never forget that exhibition of courage by Bradley. I'll never forget that game for another reason. I think it was the making of Bradley. And the making of the Knicks.

We had to go with eight players that night. We had to go with nine players for the rest of the season it soon turned out. Jackson went back to New York and eventually had spinal fushion. Then we lost Cazzie for the rest of the season when he broke his ankle.

It happened four games after the all-star break or four games after that night in San Diego. We were playing Seattle in the Garden and there were two seconds left in the third period. Cazzie sneaked downcourt and DeBusschere fired a long pass that Bob Rule deflected. Joe Kennedy of the Sonics dove for the ball and fell across Cazzie's leg. Caz went down. Whelan and I rushed out. We knew Caz was hurt badly. He was in real pain.

"It's broken, I know it's broken," he kept repeating. They carried him to the dressing room and put him on the table. Dr. Yanagisawa came in and started to probe. "Is it broken? Oh, please don't be broken," Cazzie pleaded. It was broken. "An oblique fracture of the distal right fibula," was the report from St. Clare's Hospital after X-rays.

We won the game, 113–106, but it was a depressed dressing room. Frazier cursed when he heard it was a broken bone. "Oh, no," said Bradley. It was a very costly game. The Sonics were terribly upset. "Too bad. They were going so good," said Al Bianchi, then the Seattle coach. "I don't want to mess up a guy's career. It's really very bad," said Kennedy.

Nobody felt worse than Cazzie. It was his ankle and his pain and his career. He couldn't see anything but the pain at first. But you know Caz. He has an enthusiasm that never stops bubbling.

He was in one room at St. Clare's and Jackson was across the hall. "Hey," he shouted to Phil through the door, "Let's you and me start our own wheelchair league in the hall. I'll take you on one-on-one. I get the ball first. I'm the veteran."

"I'm too busy," yelled Jackson, who was in traction. "I'm one word away from completing this puzzle. What's a six-letter word for boring?"

O

13

We lost the first game we played without Cazzie. We were beaten by the 76ers in Philadelphia in double overtime. We were leading by nine with only 1:50 to go in regulation and blew it. I sometimes wonder if any lead is safe in the NBA, even after you get into the dressing room and lock the door.

Don't laugh. It happened one night in an exhibition game with the 76ers. Cazzie hit a shot right around the buzzer. There was no doubt that it was good. We ran off the floor and to the dressing room with 113–112 victory. Philly ran off the floor with a different version. The 76ers thought the shot was late and they had won, 112–111.

So did Dave Zinkoff, the Philly announcer. He announced that Philadelphia had won. "I was all the way up the stairs and going into the dressing room when I heard the announcer say Philadelphia had won by a point," said Norm Drucker, who reffed the game with Woody Kinsbrunner, a rookie trying out. "I ran downstairs again and told the official scorer the Knicks had won." The 76ers argued but lost.

In that first game without Cazzie, we used Frazier the

entire fifty-eight minutes, his third straight complete game. Bradley worked fifty-seven minutes at forward, and Barnett and Reed played fifty-five. DeBusschere got into foul trouble, so he only played thirty-eight. I used Hosket for nineteen minutes. That was to be the pattern for the rest of the season.

Frazier, Bradley, Barnett, Reed and DeBusschere got all the playing time they could handle. The Iron Knicks, they began calling them. The others filled in whenever the situation arose. I didn't have to explain a thing to Riordan, Bowman, May and Hosket. I didn't give them any pep talks.

It is a player's responsibility to be ready all the time. I never knew when I would need them, so I couldn't tell them anything. They had to sit and stay in shape. I kept telling the guys on the bench to do some extra shooting when we had no practice. It was their responsibility. It was up to them to show how much they wanted to be part of the team.

Playing time should have nothing to do with it. I was a player and I knew what it meant not to get a game, as we used to say in Brooklyn. Everybody can't play. Not when you have twelve men on a team. Somebody has to watch. Somebody has to help when the coach determines it is needed.

That's a very important part of a ballclub. Attitude. Discipline. Unselfishness. You have to want it badly to be a real winner. That goes for the superstar or the last guy on the bench. Guys like Bradley, Riordan and Cazzie never stop practicing. They'd find a gym and a basketball in the desert.

A lot of people think pro basketball is a kid's game. That's crazy. It is hard work. It is a lot of travel. It is total dedication from the minute the players go to camp to the final minute of their last game. Yes, it can be fun and games. Yes, there are more important things in life than basketball games. But there is nothing more important than winning those basketball games if you play them.

You had to admire the way the players reacted to the loss of Cazzie and Jackson. People expected the Knicks to panic. They figured we would collapse. There was no way five players could carry such a load in the exhausting world of pro basketball. And the bench. Bowman, a discard. Riordan, who had played a couple of minutes giving fouls. May, used a few minutes in emergencies. Hosket, the same, and also with a trick knee that was to require surgery after the season.

It looked bad. But not to me. Not to Donovan. We talked about it. He said he would look around and see if there was anyone available. We agreed it wasn't necessary to get someone just to fill a uniform. I had complete faith in everyone on the team. I was not afraid to use anyone at any time.

I know it was hard for others to understand when I said I wasn't worried. The sportswriters kept pumping me. They would have had a better story if I gave them a scare reaction. I couldn't. There is no way a coach or anyone in the business of making decisions can operate with a hand that shakes. So I told everyone the same thing. "I'm going to do what I always do," I said. "I'll have a few scotches, I'll go to bed, I'll get up in the morning and I'll be thankful I'm alive."

Anytime you are here to talk about it, you are ahead of the game. There was no way of worrying Cazzie and Jackson back into uniform. In fact, those injuries did not hurt us as much as everyone seemed to think. There is no question that it helped Bradley. He had to make up Cazzie's playing time and it was like magic. It seemed to be the answer to most of Bill's problems.

Bradley stopped thinking of what he'd like to do and just went out and did it. He went back to basics. He began doing things instinctively. He got caught in the flow of the game. He relaxed. For some reason, there were no more signs of pressure, though there was more pressure on him now.

The whole team reacted the same way. It got smoother and smoother every game. Bradley, Reed, Frazier, DeBusschere and Barnett really played ball together. They read each other as though they had been playing together for years. They were a great unit. I have to believe it happened so fast because they had to play so much.

It proved that five good men could play the game and do well. But I wouldn't recommend it as a steady diet. There is no more demanding sport in the world. There are no greater atheletes in the world when you consider the nature of the game and the size, speed and coordination of the players. It would be inhuman to expect five players to play forty-eight minutes or more a game.

But the Knicks did it. We were 33-19 when Cazzie got hurt. We were 21-9 after that. With all due respect to Caz and Jackson, the only serious damage inflicted was to our room matchups. I had to get a new roomie for Frazier. His man had been Jackson. They were the Odd Couple.

They had come to me in training camp and asked if they could room toegther. They had roomed for a while as rookies the year before but that was broken up. They discovered they got along great together. They had worked out a system that fit their living habits, as with the room temperature.

Phil was from North Dakota and liked the windows open wide and the room cold. Clyde was from Atlanta and like it warm. "We've got that worked out," Jackson explained. "Clyde likes to run right out and get something

139

to eat when we get to a hotel. I'm the redcap. I've got to carry the luggage. So I get to the room first and throw open the windows as far as I can."

Jackson would freeze the room just for laughs. "Man, he likes it cold," Frazier would say. "Why, it's so cold in the room sometimes, you can see your breath." Clyde had his own devious way of getting even. He is a television nut, while Jackson is a reading nut. So the television was always on.

"I can't sleep unless the television's on," explained Frazier, who leads the team in sleeping. "The trouble is," Jackson countered, "He can turn on the television and doesn't care what's on. But I'm the kind of guy who gets hooked on a show when I look at television, which is not often. He falls asleep and snores while I'm up all hours watching a lousy show I didn't want to watch in the first place."

They also worked out an arrangement about who answers the telephone, who gets up first, who goes into the bathroom first and things like that. On the road, Danny Whelan leaves two calls for everyone on the rooming list. One is for wake-up. The other is half an hour later for guys who go back to sleep.

Jackson and Frazier had no problem. "As soon as the first call comes," explained Phil, "Clyde's out of bed, takes his shower and shaves, then he wakes me up. Clyde's always downstairs ten minutes ahead of time. He wants to beat the fine. I'm last in the room and it's up to me to see nothing's left. I check the closets, the drawers, under the bed. I'm the one who always has the problem. Clyde packs everything before he goes to bed. I wait to the last minute."

Once in a while Phil would find a shirt or some shoes. Always his. Except for one time in Vancouver. We had played the Sonics the night before and were bussing it back to Seattle. Everyone had checked in and the bus door was about to close. "Hold it," shouted a voice from the rear. It belonged to Frazier.

Clyde never stopped to explain. He ran out of the bus and into the hotel. He was gone for only a few minutes. He climbed back on the bus with a pair of alligator shoes in his hand. "Give Danny five," I informed him. "It's worth it, Red," said Frazier. "These shoes cost me a hundred dollars, so I figure I just made ninety-five."

We have no special rules about rooming on the Knicks. I try and put guys together who get along with each other. With Willis, I try and give him a small roomie. I like to give Reed a rookie. He has a lot of patience. And if the rookie knows what is good for him, he'll wait on Willis.

Like Johnny Warren. He got along great with Willis. He would run down for sandwiches and milk shakes. He would be there to carry some of the captain's packages. I remember one time in Los Angeles. Management out there did not put beer in the dressing rooms and only gave us soda. But we like beer, so Danny Whelan would send out for six-packs and we would lug them to the arena.

Whelan couldn't carry the beer and asked Warren to help. "I can't," said John. "I've got my bag and this package to carry." Reed was listening. He looked at his young roomie. "Rookie," said Willis, sweetly. "The man didn't ask what you're carrying. He asked you to carry the beer. So carry the beer." Warren carried the beer.

Bellamy, when he was with the team, always wanted to room by himself. He was a big guy and it would give him more room to move around. When he left, I'd let Bowman room alone whenever he was the odd man. Only superstars get that treatment. Nate felt good about that. When Dave Stallworth returned to the Knicks, he and Bowman roomed together because they were close from the days when they played ball at Wichita State.

Bradley roomed with Komives until the trade and then I moved him in with DeBusschere. It was a matchup made in heaven, I guess. Dave had some rough edges and Bill had the Ivy League image. They got along well. DeBusschere made Bradley such a beer drinker, Bill even began stashing a few cans in his equipment bag after the game as the other players did.

We were lucky. We had players who got along. They really pulled together after Cazzie and Jackson got hurt. We ran off eleven straight in one stretch and found ourselves in second place. We had won twenty-eight of our last thirty-two. Baltimore was first and was to wind up that way—a remarkable thing in view of the Bullets' last-place finish the season before.

We were creating our own excitement. People were talking of our team ball. They were saying the Knicks were playing basketball the way it should be played. It was nice talk. But we still spent the rest of the season trying to catch the Bullets.

We didn't even finish second. Philadelphia did. But we were satisfied to a degree. We wound up winning fifty-four games and no team in Knicks history had won more than forty-seven. It was encouraging, that's all. No more than that.

The finish was Baltimore, Philadelphia, New York and Boston. That sent us into the playoffs against the Bullets. We had taken the season series, 4-3, and were 4-1 since the DeBusschere trade and that was encouraging. The Bullets were hurting and that was encouraging. But playing Baltimore at any time never is anything but rough.

Wes Unseld had just been named Rookie of the Year and Most Valuable Player. Only Chamberlain had ever accomplished that, so Unseld was exceptional. He had a great year off the boards and playing defense and triggering the fast breaks with his fantastic passes. I never saw anyone whip the ball so far and accurately with two hands the way he does. He just puts it over his head and zings it.

Unseld was trouble. So were Monroe, Loughery, Jack Marin and Ray Scott. The Bullets had gotten a bad break when Gus Johnson tore ligaments in his knee in their fifty-sixth game and was lost for the season. Poor Gus. He always seemed to be hurt when the playoffs were on.

Loughery had some groin problem when our series started but he's a real pro. He took some shots and managed to play every game despite pain. It turned out there weren't many games. Only four. That amazed me. No one in his right mind would have predicted four straight for either New York or Baltimore.

Shue tried to surprise us in the first game by having Unseld bring the ball down. Gene wanted to get Reed away from the boards. He also wanted Willis to work more—make him come out and meet Wes and maybe even get into foul trouble.

It was fine with us if Unseld stayed outside. All we did was have DeBusschere or Reed, the closest, pick up Wes. The other would stay inside and protect the middle and the board. "Willis is the backbone of that team," Shue explained. "The more we make him work, the better we'll be in the last quarter. We'd like to see a tired competitor then."

Willis played forty-two minutes and did not tire. Monroe had a big game as usual, thirty-two points, but our defense shut off the other guys. We won, 113–101. DeBusschere wound up with twenty-one rebounds and Frazier hit eleven of eighteen shots and Barnett nine of seventeen. The Pearl said he didn't think Unseld would be bringing the ball down in the next game.

143

He was right. This time Shue had something different. He put Monroe on Bradley and Marin on Frazier. This time Barnett broke out with a beautiful game. Dick got twenty-seven points and played forty-four minutes of tough defense besides. Monroe hit twenty-nine but Frazier had a big game with twenty-three points, seven rebounds, twelve assists and a lot of steals. We held them under one hundred. We won, 107–91.

Game three in Baltimore and Shue went back to the kind of game that had won the Eastern Division title. He had Monroe back on Frazier. Still no good. We won, 119–116. It was Reed this time with thirty-five points and nineteen rebounds. Clyde had twenty-six points, seven rebounds and seventeen assists. "They're playing better basketball than we are," asknowledged Loughery, who had been slightly remarkable, himself. His groin still bothered him but he pushed himself forty-six minutes and scored twenty-nine points.

"They're an incredible team," Scott said of the Knicks. "There's no key man," said Unseld. "At first I thought it was Frazier and we all know what Reed is. Then DeBusschere. Today, it was Bradley if you ask me." He had a point.

In the second game, Bradley had grabbed thirteen rebounds, ten off the offensive board, with Monroe playing him. In the third game, Shue switched Marin back to Bill and Bradley hit ten of twelve shots. "Unbelievable," said Marin, who found out he couldn't give Bradley an inch of room. "It's unbelievable the way they hit the open man. All I did was try and help out a little when Frazier drives the middle and that was it."

It was all over two nights later in the Garden. Shue tried something else. He switched guard assignments. This time Loughery played Frazier and Monroe played Barnett. "We wanted Barnett to handle the ball and take it to the corner," the Baltimore coach explained. "Lough-ery overplayed Frazier to keep the ball from him and it worked."

Loughery supplied an interesting addition to that. "We tried to keep the ball from Frazier because he had it 90 per cent of the time the last game," said Kevin. "But then the ball went to Willis." Reed took twenty-nine shots and canned fifteen. "Generally, one guy doesn't see the ball that much on this team," said Reed, half-apologizing for all his shots, "but they kept giving it to me." A good team should be able to adjust.

We had just one scare. DeBusschere almost passed out on the bench. You know how he plays. So intense. He doesn't know how to pace himself. It's all out. He played himself into severe cramps above both knees. We were leading, 108–99, with 2:31 to go, when he signaled he wanted out.

I sent Hosket in. Dave limped to the bench. "Hold me, I think I'm going to pass out," he said to Bowman. Nate grabbed a cup of water. DeBusschere's head wobbled as he drank. It looked serious. A minute later he was back in the game. He said he had just gotten dehydrated. That's DeBusschere.

We won, 115–108, and once more demonstrated we had a team all the way down the bench. Frazier picked up his fourth personal in the third period and I sent in May. I switched Bradley backcourt and put Donnie at forward. He hit 4-for-7 and had six rebounds and three assists for twenty-one minutes. He handled the pressure with no problem.

Nobody had ever swept a division winner before and we did it. We felt great. Baltimore felt terrible. It wasn't necessary. They still scare a lot of our players more than any other team in the league. I'm sure if Gus Johnson had played it might have been a little different.

"I don't see any reason why the Knicks can't win it all," said Shue, referring to the NBA title. "They play real good defense. They have a lot of good open shooters. They are great competitors. And they have Willis Reed." He overlooked only one thing. A little thing like Bill Russell.

Russell and the Celtics had finished fourth in the East but then went on to beat Philadelphia, 4-1. They were supposed to be the old men of Boston who finally had it. We had seen Russell taken to the hospital after a game with us in Boston near the end of the season. He had hit the floor hard after stuffing a shot but it was sheer fatigue more than anything else that caused him to lay there.

They carried him to the dressing room and he broke down and cried from emotional exhaustion. They tried to keep him in the hospital a few days but he managed to get his clothes and somehow sneak out. He was back in uniform when the playoffs started and helped destroy the 76ers. They should have locked him in an isolation ward and thrown the key away.

They beat us in six games. Or Bill Russell beat us in six games. Em Bryant, our Em Bryant, didn't help us. He was the difference in the game we lost on our floor to open the series. He played forty minutes and had eleven rebounds and six assists and ran the attack. It was a bad game to lose. We blew the whole series by not winning that one. But it never could have happened if not for Russell.

He played the whole game and kept the pressure on us all the time. We had been beating the Celtics by charging right out and pressing them all over the place. But we were flat at the start. We didn't get off. They did. They got in front by fifteen. We closed to within 78–73 but they won, 108–100. "We weren't sharp," said Frazier. "Maybe it was the three-day layoff since the Baltimore series. When I take thirty-one shots, we can't win. I don't take that many in practice."

We were just horrible in the second game. Or, looking at it from Boston's viewpoint, Russell was terrific. Our guys spent too much time looking for him under the boards. Would you believe we missed thirty of thirty-three shots in one stretch and wound up with 9-for-47 at half time? We lost 112–97 and the only nice thing that happened was that I gave Cazzie Russell a chance to play a few minutes.

Caz had made a remarkably fast recovery from his broken ankle but was to be no real influence in the series. We won the third game at home, 101–91, but we never got over losing the first two games. The Celtics won up there, 97–96, and that was really it. We came so close in that one.

Bryant, that little pest, didn't treat his old teammates or his pal Willis Reed very well at all. Once he cutely raced Frazier to a spot and drew a charging call that wiped out Clyde's basket. Another time he came up with a big rebound out of a scramble. Then, with six seconds to go, he hit two foul shots that were the difference.

"You can see the crest of the hill from here," crowed Em, the pest, after Boston took a 3-1 lead. We won the fifth game in New York, 112–104, but Frazier pulled a groin muscle that was to limit his mobility and time for the final game in Boston. It ended for us when the Celtics took the sixth game, 106–105.

Boston went on to win the NBA championship in a last hurrah for Bill Russell and Sam Jones. We went home to wait for another year. "I'm disappointed," said Bradley. "I don't want to stop now. It's fun." The players vowed, right there in Boston, they would win it next season.

O

14

Something happened the night the Knicks eliminated the Baltimore Bullets from the 1968-69 playoffs in four straight that was more important than any ball game. Eddie Donovan gave me the news about Dave Stallworth —that the doctors had told The Rave he could try and play.

Stallworth had come to New York for his routine examination. He dropped by the dressing room in the Garden that night to chat with the fellows. He never said a word about his situation because he did not know at the time. He left the dressing room with Donovan. They went to Dr. Yanagisawa's office down the hall.

That's when The Rave got the word. That's when Dr. Yanagisawa told Stallworth his heart condition had improved and he probably could play, again. He was asked not to say anything but Stalls could not resist. "They've told me my heart's healed," he informed a newspaper friend.

Who could blame him for not keeping a secret like that. He had been through plenty. Basketball was his whole life and it was all lost when he suffered the symptoms of

148

a heart attack while the Knicks were playing San Francisco in Fresno on March 7, 1967. It was later given the medical term "myocardial infarction." According to the dictionary, an infarct is "a circumscribed portion of tissue which has suddenly been deprived of its blood supply by embolism or thrombosis and, which as a result, is undergoing death to be replaced by scar tissue."

Dick McGuire was the coach at the time and Stallworth had complained of chest pains. McGuire took him out of the game and sent him to the dressing room. "I made a basket, a left-handed hook shot," recalled Stallworth, "when I felt a knot in my chest." He had never had it before. The Knicks had played in Los Angeles the night before and Stalls had been fine.

They took no chances. Stalls did not play the rest of the game against San Francisco and went to a Fresno hospital for a cardiograph. They found nothing. He immediately flew on to San Francisco for a game the following night. He stayed in bed at the Jack Tar Hotel until noon. "I feel fine," he said. "Nothing bothers me. My chest doesn't hurt anymore."

He was not worried about a heart attack. He was ready to play that night. McGuire wasn't so sure. No coach is going to fool around with anything like that. A coach is not a doctor. McGuire did the right thing. He had a doctor look at Stallworth. It was the same doctor who had accompanied Stalls to the hospital in Fresno for the cardiograph, so he knew the situation. "I was afraid to let him play," said Dick. He wasn't even sure about letting Stalls play after the doctor had said it would be okay. "You can play but if you have any signs of distress, get right out," the doctor cautioned Stallworth.

Stallworth played and lasted ten minutes. He got kicked in the thigh by Nate Thurmond while driving to the basket and had to leave. Who knows what might have happened if he had continued? We know this. When he got back to New York the next day, a Monday, he went right into the hospital for extensive tests. That's when they discovered his condition and he was told he could never play again.

That didn't stop him. Stallworth began sneaking in some basketball back in Wichita as soon as he had a chance. It was about a year after he got out of the hospital. At first, his friends wouldn't let him play. "They were more afraid for me than I was," he said. "They'd make me shoot down at one end while they played."

He never accepted the fact that he was through with basketball. Even while he was in the hospital, he kept saying he didn't believe it. He never told anyone, but the son-of-a-gun was scheming all along. I can understand. Stallworth is a bundle of enthusiasm. He is a free-wheeler in every respect. He is running through life and enjoying it his way. He wants to be part of the action.

He has a great attitude about things. The Knicks kept him on the payroll and he went back to Wichita and pretty soon he began exercising. First it was golf. Then it was shooting baskets. Then it was one-on-one and two-on-two. Then he coached an amateur team named the Wichita Builders. He also sneaked in some playing time.

He must have known something the doctors didn't know. He would come to New York for his regular examinations and then go home and play basketball without telling anyone. "Deep within me I felt physically able to play," he explained. "If anything happened, and there was a chance to play again, I was going to take it." He kept coming to New York for reassurance that his heart condition had not gotten worse.

Yet, it was inconceivable then, and is still inconceivable to me that Stallworth could ever play again. How could anyone play pro basketball, of all sports, after a heart attack? It's enough to make you nervous just to think of it, even when you know that heart specialists had cleared Stallworth and let him come to our training camp on opening day.

"Everyone is afraid but me," he said. He was right. Well, not exactly afraid. Call it a funny feeling. I still get it when I see him hit the floor and lie there. Stallworth hits the floor a lot and lies there a lot. He plays all-out and likes to grab a rest on the house once in a while. It's scary, though.

The doctors still watch him carefully. He undergoes periodic examinations. He has been advised to report any discomfort and to report any chest or stomach pain. I still can't get over the way he dives for free balls and hits the boards with the big men and runs like hell on a fast break. He's a remarkable young man in many ways and it didn't take a heart attack to prove it to us.

We knew the kind of person he was when we drafted him. We knew he was an effervescent individual and a great team player. We knew he didn't need sympathy to help him get along. He had struggled to get where he was and he wasn't about to give up without a fight.

"I just made up my mind to be ready to play and do my job when the opportunity came," he said. He felt that way about basketball and he felt that way after rejoining the Knicks and finding things somewhat established. We had just come through a season where five players finished up doing most of the work. He had been away almost two and a half years and it was not going to be that easy.

We were all rooting for him. Deep down there was some apprehension, but not with Stallworth. He had won his freedom. "I don't have to live in fear the rest of my life," he said when he reported to Farmingdale. "I had fears for the first year. They told me I should feel tired and I never felt that. They said I should have dizzy spells

151

and black out and that never happened. When they told me I was going back to camp, I felt like I could jump over a building."

Stallworth fit right in from the start. It was as though he never was away. His timing was off but he still had the same old enthusiasm and drive. We didn't pamper him. That wouldn't have helped him or us. He had to find out about himself and we had to find out about him.

He had to go all-out to prove to everyone, and possibly himself, that he no longer had to live in fear. It was a great feeling to watch him frolicking out there like a yearling. After a while, we stopped thinking and noticing and that's when the comeback really came true. It's still slightly unbelievable to this day.

It was a strange feeling the first time he played in an exhibition game down in Salem, Virginia, against the Baltimore Bullets. It was a wild occasion the first time he played a regular season game in front of the Garden fans. "Number nine . . . Dave Stallworth," was the way announcer John Condon introduced The Rave. Just like that, there were 14,796 fans on their feet—yelling, applauding, whistling. All of us on the Knick bench joined in. You couldn't help it.

"I was embarrassed," Stallworth told us. "I didn't expect anything like that. Maybe a generous hand but not that." The young man not only is modest but has a sense of humor to match. I used him fourteen minutes and he was hectic, as usual. He shot 4-for-7, he got six rebounds and handed off for two assists. We beat Seattle, 126–101. "I thought the team played extremely well and I played fair," The Rave said.

Stallworth was fascinated by what was going on. The league was strange to him in a sense. A lot of things can change in two and a half years. Like Lew Alcindor, for

example. Stalls knew about Alcindor. He had heard all the
same stories as everyone.

We were all intrigued by Lew. Some of the Knicks had
played against him in the Maurice Stokes game at the
Kutsher's Country Club in Monticello. Reed and Frazier
were really impressed. Little did they realize at the time
that it was going to be the last Stokes game for Maurice
and Joe Lapchick.

Stokes had been attending the game for a few years.
They would fly him in a private plane from Cincinnati
and he would go right back to the hospital. He would sit
and watch from his wheelchair on the sidelines and then
hand gifts to the players. They would kid him and he
would chuckle.

This time most of the people turned out to see Alcindor against Chamberlain, the only one who had played in
all the Stokes games. Wilt had traveled from Los Angeles
for his eleventh appearance. One time he even came in
from Europe to help raise money for Maurice. At his own
expense.

Alcindor made a few moves against Wilt that turned
on some of the NBA guys. "The man's good, that's all
there is to it," said Chamberlain after sampling Lew's
quickness. "It's tough enough that he's seven feet tall,"
said Ray Scott, "but to be beaten by his quickness, that's
something else."

Frazier went way out on the limb. He predicted Alcindor would break Chamberlain's record of one hundred
points in a game. Walt came to training camp with stories
about Lew's nonchalance. He said he was a real pro. We
found out more about that the night we played Milwaukee
in an exhibition game in the Garden.

Alcindor played only twenty minutes because of a bad
ankle and fouled out with 7:26 to go. "I can outplay him,"
said Willis, after we lost, 120–118, "but it's a hard night's

153

work." What seemed to surprise Reed was when Alcindor went over him once to grab a rebound and stick it back in.

I would say that Lew's speed is what impresssed me the most. He had great reflexes for a guy his size. I realized right away that Willis would have to make him work hard and not let him stand around and do what he wanted. That's always a good tactic against any big man. You must keep him moving.

We saw enough in one night to tell us that Alcindor would be a tremendous influence in the league for years to come. We didn't need Guy Rodgers to remind us. But he did. "I've played with a lot of big guys," said little Guy, "but I've never seen a guy that quick and knowledgeable. He's faster than Thurmond and has a greater variety of shots than Nate and Wilt. I don't think anyone has seen the real Alcindor yet."

I hope we never do. The one we faced in his first year was enough. He made Milwaukee a tougher club. He made the Bucks a contender. They rated right up there, and we were in a tough division. You would never know it the way people talked. Someone even came up to me one day and suggested we would go unbeaten.

There seemed to be a lot of excitement about the Knicks. I had to shut off practice at camp once in a while to get some work done. We kept working mostly on defense but this time there was not that much work with the press. We didn't have Jackson to apply the pressure and the press was not that good without him.

Cazzie was back, his ankle perfectly healed. We broke in Stallworth to play behind DeBusschere. We had only one addition to the team that had finished the season in the playoffs with Boston. Besides Stallworth, that is. We had drafted Johnny Warren of St. John's as our top pick.

There were no radical changes. Cazzie fit neatly as the sixth man behind Reed, Frazier, Barnett, Bradley and

DeBusschere. Our bench had gotten some playing time and Riordan, Bowman, May and Hosket were more familiar with our defense. Hosket was coming off knee surgery and reported a little overweight but that was understandable.

Everyone was in camp early and ready. You could sense they realized they had a good shot at going all the way. I guess DeBusschere was the best example. He worked with a doctor all summer to get his weight down. That's the first time he ever did that. He would blow up to 260. We wanted him to come in at 240. We felt he would be better off with less weight the way he played.

DeBusschere reported to training ready to play. I wasn't thinking about the league or other teams. I let them know we would be scrimmaging the first day and we were not going to waste any time getting anyone in shape. I wanted to get certain things done. I wanted to lay a foundation right away. We had a lot of work to do on helping out and double teaming.

A lot of teams play themselves into shape. I don't believe in that. That's a waste of time. Our players had to be ready. We only had seven or eight days in training camp. You only are allowed twenty-eight days by the Players' Association and you have to play exhibitions. You can play twelve but we only play ten. I think ten is enough. It gives us time between games to go back and review things that way.

I worked a little extra with Stallworth on defense. I sat with him and reviewed everything. We practiced twice a day, one and a half hours each time. Our first practice would start at eleven and we'd break for lunch. Then we'd be back at five.

I don't like sessions too close and I don't think ballplayers should get up early in training camp. The guys got to have a chance to relax. It was tough in our camp. Right away, the magazines and authors began showing up. We hadn't done a thing yet but they were there.

Not that I minded. They had a job to do and we do have an obligation to cooperate with the media. But where does it begin and end? Especially when some people walk right in and expect certain privileges we don't even extend to the newspapermen who cover us every day.

One day in Boston, for example, a television guy came into our dressing room and wanted to take a shower. Another time in Philadelphia, a guy walked in and went right to the toilet. I asked him who he was. He gave me some double-talk. I told him to get out. Don't you think the same guy showed up a year later and did the same thing?

Our dressing room is open to all legitimate members of the news media. We never keep it closed more than a minute or two, win or lose. I don't think there is anything you have to say that takes longer than that. If it is very serious, it can keep until you can take all the time you need.

We have newspapermen who travel with us and work every game. Time is important to them and they deserve consideration. They represent the public. If we lock out the press, we are locking out the cash customers. That is why the Knicks never have kept their dressing room closed. And that was the case long before I got there.

It did get a little crowded. Frazier had an author. De-Busschere had an author. The Knicks had an author. Everyone seemed to be an author or guy writing a special article. They even interviewed our ballboys. They all had problems. All I had ahead of me was eighty-two games and the responsibility of trying to win a championship.

We managed to work things out so we could practice and play our games without too much chaos. We even managed to have a wedding before the season started. May got married between exhibition games. "I'm still happily married," he said when he reported back a few days later.

So were the Knicks. We worked to get off fast and we did. We won our first five and then lost at home to San Francisco in a game that will take a long time to forget. Thurmond was thrown out in the first nineteen minutes yet we were beaten, 112–109. Jake O'Donnell hit him with a technical, then chased him. "I said something bad," big Nate confessed.

Jeff Mullins hurt us with his shooting for a change. But what I think happened is what always happens under conditions like that: one team lets up because it looks easy and the other tries harder because it looks tougher. The defeat really didn't mean much at the time. But then we went out and won our next eighteen.

Now, there is something I'll never forget. You start a winning streak like that and at first it really doesn't mean anything but more victories. Pretty soon people start noticing that you've got nine and ten and eleven. Then they rush to the record books, and the writers start writing and the players begin thinking.

It all started innocently enough in Detroit, the game after we lost to San Francisco. Our defense was superb. DeBusschere and Reed were superb. They kept intercepting passes. They never gave the Pistons a chance. Butch van Breda Kolff tried everything. He even used McCoy McLemore, a 6-6 forward, against Reed. We won, 116–92.

It was a good game for us and a bad one for the Pistons. Most of the talk in the dressing room was about Jerry Lucas. He had just been traded to San Francisco by Cincinnati for Bill Turner and Jim King. "I wish we could've gotten Lucas," said Dave Bing, who was recovering from minor knee surgery at the time.

We had a great game in the Garden against Baltimore. We beat the Bullets, 128–99. We applied pressure on the ball handlers and the fellows helped out in deep. Gus Johnson got only nine shots and was upset. "The guards are controlling the ball too much," he insisted. It depends on the viewpoint. Our players liked to think they had something to do with it.

We heard a tremendous roar in the last minute. We couldn't imagine what it was since we were way ahead. We finally discovered the fans were rooting for us to hold the Bullets under one hundred points. It became a ritual. I didn't really like it because I realized how the other players felt, but there was nothing I could do about it.

We were 7-1 and the players were really enjoying it. Winning does that, for some reason. Cazzie seemed to be having the most fun. He had taken eight shots in nine minutes against Baltimore and made three. "Sh," he said to those around him, while blowing on his shooting hand. "I'm still hot. You got to get it while you can. The pace is fast and furious. You might as well shoot when you can."

Everyone laughed. Caz then turned to our rookie, John Warren. He had made a jumper for his only basket in two tries. "John Warren," said Caz. "You shot from the corner with two men on you. I think I was open." I had little to say to the newspapermen. The players took care of that quite adequately.

We kept on winning. Three in a row were by twenty-four over the Atlanta Hawks in the Garden, and Guerin said some nice things again. "The most impressive thing I saw," he said, "was when they were up by twenty-five, they worked like it was a close game. They applied the pressure on defense and didn't get selfish and played team ball." We won, 128–104.

Number four was by thirteen over San Diego in the Garden and Frazier got forty-three points. He also got some ovation. It lasted about two minutes. "It was a helluva tribute," he told the newspapermen. "They start to clap and then it builds up. I started to stand up and bow. I wanted to do something. I was going to stand up and start yelling; 'We're Number One'."

I apologized to him for not putting him back when the crowd yelled "We want Clyde." "That's all right, Red," he said. "I missed enough easy shots while I was out there." Good old Clyde. Fast with words and fast with his hands.

We escaped with number five against Milwaukee by four points. We won, 112–108, in the Garden, but Rodgers had a shot at a tie with seven seconds to go and Bradley put it away with two fouls. I was impressed with the coaching job Larry Costello had done. The Bucks had used the zone press very well. Alcindor only got thirty-six points and twenty-seven rebounds. Flynn Robinson fired thirty-four. What more can I say?

Reed was a little embarrassed by Alcindor's performance. Not that it was Willis's fault. We play a team defense and it is geared for Reed to get help against an Alcindor. It didn't work well that night. The next time it did. We played the Bucks in Milwaukee in our next game. "I stunk," said Lew after we won, 109–93, for six in a row. Willis had something to do with it.

There was one critical period and Reed took charge. We kept going to Willis because he was moving Alcindor in and out and overpowering him. The Bucks were within seven points, but Willis put together four quick baskets and it was over. Reed had learned something about the 7-2 center.

For one thing, Willis insisted Alcindor was at least 7-4. And very, very agile. "I can't just take the ball and stand around and jump over him," said Reed. "He's too big. I don't really concentrate on him, anyway. I'm not out to prove I'm a bigger man. I don't put out more against him than anyone else. We needed the ball game."

So Willis muscled Alcindor and we all got the job done. The game before we needed help from Bowman. Nate the Snake hit six of his eleven shots, grabbed eight rebounds, blocked three shots, stole three passes intended for Alcindor and got a standing ovation. That's the way we were going. Everyone was helping.

We kept winning and the streak kept growing, but we paid little attention. What looked nice after we won in Phoenix, 116–99, for seven straight was the 12-1 in the standings. Cazzie gave us a scare. He hurt his back in the first half. I told him to get dressed at half time and he watched the rest of the game from the bench.

We went to San Diego the next day and sent him to Dr. Paul Bauer. He was the same doctor who diagnosed Phil Jackson's back as a spinal problem that would require surgery. "I hope it's not like Phil," said Cazzie. It wasn't. It was a routine muscle spasm.

Cazzie decided to sleep on the floor for a while. "It only hurts when I sneeze or laugh," he said. "I sneezed this morning and almost went through the ceiling. And that Barnett. He has that dry sense of humor and he makes me laugh. I've got to make him stop."

There was real grief in San Diego when we got there. The papers were full of stories about Elvin Hayes and Don Kojis. The Big E was quoted as saying he did not like the way Kojis was picking on him. Hayes wanted to be traded. The guy in the middle was Jack McMahon.

His team was losing and his superstar was unhappy. That's a pretty tough parlay. McMahon knew it. Owner Bob Breitbard had told Hayes he never would be traded. The loss to us was the Rockets' eighth straight. They were last in the West with 1-9. General manager Pete Newell was quoted as saying the coach was safe but the players weren't.

"I know coaches get fired," said McMahon. "In my first

year at Cincinnati, I was fifty-five and twenty-two and there were stories about me getting fired." He recalled how Andy Phillip had the St. Louis Hawks in first place with a 6-4 record but he was let out by Ben Kerner. Someone asked Benny why. "They didn't look good," was the answer.

McMahon didn't last long after that episode. He was replaced by Alex Hannum, an old buddy. Another thing happened while we were in San Diego. In fact, we were in the early minutes of our game with the Rockets when we got word that Chamberlain had ripped his knee and had undergone surgery. We were shocked. For some reason you never want to believe news like that. It just didn't seem possible that it could happen to Wilt. He seemed so impregnable to everybody. That's all we talked about after the game. "What if anything happened to me and Willis?" suggested DeBusschere. I felt like biting his tongue.

Los Angeles was our next stop and Chamberlain was in the hospital when we got there. The tendons that hold the kneecap like guy wires had snapped and had to be repaired, yet he said he would be back before the season ended. Everyone laughed. The doctors said it was impossible.

"He tried to psych us with that story about coming back so fast," said Frazier. " 'I shall return.' He sounds like General MacArthur. But if I know Wilt, he'll probably be back fast. He's probably practicing his free throws right now in his bed."

Joe Mullaney used Rick Roberson, a 6-9 rookie from Cincinnati University, in Wilt's place. He did a good job against Reed and a fine job on DeBusschere. Or Dave's nose. Rick broke it. DeBusschere had to play the next few games with an aluminum protection taped over his nose.

Roberson wore himself out trying to stop Reed. He did

161

well until he tired. Willis wound up with thirty-five points and sixteen rebounds, and we harassed Jerry West into thirteen misses on eighteen tries. We let Barnett pressure him and the other guys helped when he needed it. You always need help against West, no matter who is on him. No one man can stop Jerry. He is an incredible shooter. He is an incredible basketball player.

Jerry went to the line eighteen times that night and hit eighteen but it was worth it. Any team would be happy to give him a shot at one point all night if he just wouldn't do anything else. We won our ninth in a row, 112–102, and Cazzie didn't play. I had a hunch the Lakers missed Wilt, too.

By the time we got to San Francisco, the Warriors were the only team we had not beaten. The record books were open and someone discovered that 16-1 was the best NBA start ever. We were 14-1 going into San Francisco. We were 15-1 coming out. We won, 116–103, and it was our defense again. We were ahead by only four entering the last period but we held them to eighteen points, which is tough when you have shooters like Mullins, Thurmond and Lucas.

The players were playing unselfish ball and show me a coach who doesn't like that. They were playing hard, as though every game was the World Series, and we were really only starting the season. There was no one outstanding player. They all contributed. Willis even donated his upper plate in San Francisco. Someone broke it.

"Moms Mabley," chirped Barnett as Willis stood in the middle of the dressing room biting his gums. Reed glared. Everyone broke up. Even I smiled. It was a good feeling to see the way the players got along. Reed was playing great ball and they appreciated it.

So did a lot of players around the league. West said some nice things about Willis in Los Angeles. "He's by far the outstanding player in the league right now," said Jerry. "He is so mobile and so strong and he can shoot. And he plays strong defense."

DeBusschere was remarkable the way he played with that gruesome object taped to his nose. He got sixteen of his twenty-four points and ten of his twelve rebounds in the second half against San Francisco and he had to have trouble breathing. Bradley, his roomie, made a big fuss about it in the dressing room. "He sleeps quieter now," said Bill. "He used to snore. It's the only reason why I'm glad he has a broken nose."

We beat Chicago next, 114–99, in the Garden and then the Boston Celtics, 113–98, and we had ourselves a record. We were 17-1 and the old NBA record was 16-1 set by the Washington Caps of 1948.

The players weren't particularly interested in that record. They talked about the Celtics and the trouble they were in. They kidded Bradley about the elbow he threw and the shoulder he jammed into Bailey Howell. He was Bad Bill. It was twelve in a row for us and seven in a row for Boston. How times had changed.

Frazier was growing his mustache again. He had shaved it off earlier in the season. No special reason. He just decided it should go. Now it was coming back. No special reason. Clyde said he woke up one morning and looked in the mirror and didn't recognize himself. Thus the mustache. And the sideburns. I didn't care if he had hair down to his toes if he kept playing the way he was playing.

We beat Cincinnati, 112–94, in the Garden for our thirteenth straight and everyone wanted to know what was going on with Oscar Robertson. The newspapermen asked if I had noticed how the Cincinnati players had kept the ball away from him. Why would Norm Van Lier and Fred Foster and Herm Gilliam handle the ball with Oscar on the floor? I gave standard answer number forty-two: I shrugged.

They went to Frazier. "Very surprising, he was never in the game," said Clyde, most obligingly. They went to Reed. "The way they're playing, it's not their style of basketball," he said. They went to Oscar. "No comment," was his first answer. "Ask the coach. That's all I can say," was his second.

They asked Bob Cousy. "I'm trying to get more players involved in the offense," he explained. "I've told the players not to look for Oscar all the time, but if they're in trouble look for him." Who ever said a basketball coach has a soft job?

We got away with a tough one in Philadelphia for our fourteenth straight. We escaped, 98–94, I do mean escaped. We were leading, 96–94, with five second left when the 76ers called time out. Ramsay is a shrewd guy. I knew he was cooking up something in his huddle. Cunningham had just scored a big basket and I figured he had to be involved. I told the players to watch Billy and Greer. Pretty smart, eh?

They knew what I meant without going into much detail in the minute we had. But I reminded them, anyway. Cunningham and Greer were to be overplayed by their men, and the other guys had to be ready to help out. Ramsay was thinking with me. He put in a variation of the play on which Cunningham had just scored.

Billy was to come out like he was getting the ball but would set a pick for Greer instead. We didn't know it at the time. We found out later. At least I found out later. DeBusschere spotted it right away. He saw Darrall Imhoff line up differently than on the play when Cunningham shot. Dave told Bradley to watch the middle, figuring that's where they were setting the screen for the shooter.

When the pass came in, Bradley dropped off his man, Matt Guokas, and went to the top of the key. Sure enough, Greer got the pass and turned for his jumper. Bradley was right on him. The shot was deflected. DeBusschere had saved the game by being so alert. The 76ers were stunned when they heard Dave had read the play.

"How did DeBusschere know that?" asked Cunningham. "It was the first time we ever used that play. He's a sneak. He goes down and listens in our huddle. He's cheating. Tell him I said that." That DeBusschere will make a good coach someday—again.

I thought back to the time when I first took over the team and how I knew I had to get everyone involved. This was a great example of team contribution. DeBusschere didn't depend on the coach to do all the thinking. A coach is only part of a team. I encourage all suggestions. I want the players to discuss their ideas openly. They do and I'm not afraid to accept anything that will help.

We were getting close to a real record now—seventeen victories in a row. Even I began noticing though I didn't talk about it. I don't believe in making any game something special. Every one is important enough to win. But when you've won fourteen in a row and the record's seventeen, I must confess the coach has to be made of iron not to notice it. Or he shouldn't read the papers or talk to reporters or his publicity men.

Frankie Blauschild and Jimmy Wergeles of our publicity department never would let me overlook a thing like that. You can imagine what they were like when we took care of Phoenix in the Garden, 128–114, and had fifteen straight. I was glad the players weren't feeling the pressure of winning.

They were 20-1 and acting like they felt they never would lose. They were tough and playing great team ball. I felt like a guy pulling strings. Some newspapermen had their fun. They began calling me a push-button coach. Everything I did was right. Thanks to the players. It was an ordeal to play against the Knicks the way we were going. "My ankles, my arms, my wrists and even my face is tired," said Connie Hawkins, the great Phoenix rookie, after he played forty-two minutes against Reed, DeBusschere and Stallworth.

Our next game was with Los Angeles in the Garden and some of the players were worried. The Lakers came in with only seven players who could play. Roberson was on the bench only because the rules require eight in uniform. DeBusschere was telling everyone how he had told his wife Geri it was the kind of game where we could get hurt. It looked too easy.

It wasn't. We finally beat them, 103–96, but we had some sweat. Jerry West got forty-one points. It looked like one hundred and eight. The Lakers actually were ahead by six in the third quarter. We wore them down but not before Joe Mullaney tried to outslick us. He isolated West against Barnett by putting his four other guys on the opposite side of the court. I told my players to play between their men and the ball, so that someone would be able to drop off and help Barnett when West got into his shooting zone.

Mendy Rudolph, the head official of the league, did not think we were in a legal defense. Mullaney reminded him, of course. "They're playing a zone!" Joe kept screaming. Mendy hit us with two technicals. He claimed we were playing an area and not our men. We disagreed. You know who won. But we won what counted—the game.

"There's only one little thing," said Frazier. "We won. they lost. It was a lousy game for us. I felt we were lucky to win. I think I heard a few boos. I guess maybe we've spoiled the fans, but they've got to realize we're only human, too." I couldn't blame people for thinking otherwise. We were playing impossible ball. To win sixteen in a row in a league like ours was just too much.

How long could it go on? It only had to continue for two more games and the Knicks would have the NBA record. The series continued in Atlanta on Thanksgiving Eve and we had some game. "If they picked out any five players in the league and put them on the court against the Knicks tonight, they couldn't have stopped them," said Guerin. We won, 138–108, and I confess I was a push-button coach.

We had some third period. I've never seen anything like it. We wouldn't let them get a shot. We kept stealing the ball. Even I sat there spellbound, with my mouth shut—relatively speaking. In the dressing room, the players had talked seriously about the record for the first time. They were so close they could touch it and they weren't going to let it get away.

Barnett ran into Bill Bridges in the toilet. Atlanta uses the Georgia Tech facilities and there is only one locker room. The Hawks use one end, the visiting team the other. Otherwise, it is communal living.

"You guys are not going to tie any records against me tonight," Bridges assured Barnett. "What's the matter, Bill," Dick said, "aren't you gonna play?"

We got our big chance in the third quarter and the only thing I can think of was the way Joe Louis used to put away a fighter he had hurt. We outscored the Hawks 38–12. It was 32–5 in the last nine minutes of the period. "That's the most embarrassing 12 minutes I've ever spent, either as a player or coach," said Guerin. "Frazier showed the best individual effort and the Knicks the best team performance I have ever seen. That Frazier stole everything but our jocks."

We flew out the next morning to Cleveland for our date with destiny. That's how they say it, don't they? We had a game there with Cincinnati. Now all the talk was about the record. We had tied Boston of 1959 and Washington of 1946 at seventeen straight. Now we were shooting to put the Knicks in the record book with eighteen.

Who will ever forget that game? I could feel tension in the dressing room for the first time. I did a little more kidding than usual. I wanted them to relax. I wanted them to feel that this was just another game. It wasn't meant to be.

How we won it, I'll never know. I've watched the films many times to refresh my memory, but always seem to forget some detail. What I do remember is Bob Cousy coming into the game with 1:49 to go. I looked it up. Oscar Robertson had fouled out and Cousy had to make a substitution. He chose himself. Imagine putting himself on a spot like that. Once a pro, always a pro.

Funny thing about Oscar fouling out. He had given two fouls early in the game and it cost him. That is why we have our bench give fouls to avoid just such a thing happening to a Frazier or Barnett or Russell. Cousy was ahead, 101–98, when he put himself in, but it still was remarkable.

Bob had been away from the game a long time. He had put on a suit only because he felt he could help the gate in Cincinnati and might help the team in a tight game somewhere along the line. You would never know he had been away at all. The first thing he did was find Van Lier with a great cross-court pass. Norm hit a jumper and that matched the basket Frazier had just scored for us.

So it was still three points. Then Cousy really amazed me. We missed a shot and they got the ball and he wound up with two shots. He stepped to the line and calmly put them both through cleanly. Five points down with a little over twenty seconds to go. I wasn't thinking of the streak. I was thinking of the game. Was it still possible to win?

168

We had gotten a real tough break just before Cousy's fouls. Reed looked like he saved a ball from going out of bounds but the officials ruled he stepped on the line. Willis didn't think so. Those are the kind of breaks that make losers, not winners. Cousy got his two shots after Cincinnati was given possession.

It was 105–100 when we took the ball out. There was no time to think. It was down to the instinctive stage. Experience, ability and training. Nothing more. Nothing less. We had to get the ball down fast, score and somehow get it back again and get three more points to tie.

We pushed it down as fast as we could. We went to Reed automatically. He was our big guy. He might drive and get a three-pointer. The Cincy guys jammed the middle. They dropped off to help with Reed. There was no chance to drive. Willis went up with a jumper and was hit by Tom Van Arsdale, who had come over to give a hand.

Cincy was in a penalty situation, so Reed got three opportunities to make two fouls. He missed the first and everyone on our bench got nervous. He had to make the next two to give us any kind of a shot at a tie. He did. It was 105–102 and sixteen seconds to go when Cousy took the ball out under his basket.

This is where some of our hard work paid off. This is where we had to apply the press on Cousy and everyone on the court. We had to get the ball back fast. Cincinnati had time and the twenty-four-second clock on its side. We pressed. Cousy had five seconds to get the ball in bounds. He couldn't find an open man. He had to call time.

That was to turn out to be a very important time-out because it was Cincinnati's last one. It didn't seem like much at the time. It enabled Cousy to escape the press and it moved the pass-in automatically to midcourt. Even if we stole the ball, we'd waste more precious time moving it downcourt than if we had picked off a pass under Cincy's basket.

We discussed things in our huddle. We weren't concerned with anyone on Cincinnati shooting. We had to cover everyone because all Cincy had to do was get the ball into someone and kill the little time that was left. There is only one thing to do in a situation like that—stay between your man and the ball. I told our guys to overplay and the deep men should be ready to help out on a lob pass. In other words, don't let anyone sneak too far behind them.

Cousy intended to go to his strength against our obvious intentions. He had been through enough of these situations to know what we were going to do. He sent Dierking back into the game for exactly that reason. He figured we'd overplay the logical receivers, so he told Connie to play deep and then come tearing out to meet the ball if everyone was trapped.

That way, Cousy could throw him a high pass that would be very tough to pick off. Reed messed it up. Willis wouldn't let Dierking come out. He blocked him off completely. Cousy was stuck with the ball at midcourt. He had no more times-out. He had to get the ball in or lose possession. He saw Van Arsdale sweeping toward him in a desperate attempt to get the pass.

That's what made Cousy such a great player. He always could see everything developing in front of him. He spotted Van rushing at him and tried to lay the ball on the floor in his path. There was no other way. He couldn't throw it directly because Riordan was pressing and had him screened out. DeBusschere had seen Cousy in trouble and anticipated Van Arsdale's move. Dave swooped in and picked off the pass and went in for a layup.

"I went to the inside of Van and took a chance," said DeBusschere. "I figured if Cousy lobbed the ball over my head, Frazier, who was overplaying Van Lier, would get a chance to pick it off." That's what makes the Knicks a good team. A coach can only remind the players what they should do. They have to do it.

We had lost only three seconds and we were within one point, 105–104. Now we had a chance to win it. We really were motivated. Our feet had wings. Cousy got the pass-in to Van Arsdale and he began dribbling up court. He had to get over midcourt by ten seconds and then Cincy only had to kill the remaining time.

Tom put on one of those typical Van Arsdale drives. DeBusschere was right with him. Riordan doubled back after pressing Cousy on the pass-in. Reed moved over. Van Arsdale ran into a triple team. I think it was Willis who slapped the ball free. Frazier picked it up. There was no chance to see how much time was left.

Now the action went the other way. Frazier dribbled. DeBusschere raced towards the basket. Van Arsdale came rushing back. Clyde stopped at the head of the key for a jumper. He missed but the rebound came right back to him. Clyde got another shot and this time he was fouled by Van Arsdale.

Walt had a 3-for-2. He didn't need it. He made two in a row cleanly with two seconds to go. Cincy still had a chance to win it, of course, but Reed picked off the throw-in and it was all over, though we did get a little scare when Willis barrelled into Van Lier. There was no time left. Frazier made sure of that by pointing to the clock when the ref was considering an offensive foul.

Since an offensive foul is not a shooting foul, and since there was no time left, anyway, the ref signaled the game was over. We had won eighteen in a row. Our record was now 23-1. "Beautiful, beautiful," Bradley kept saying in our rather wild dressing room.

It was beautiful. It still is beautiful every time I get a chance to see the replay of the telecast. I can still hear announcer Bob Wolfe saying: "Whatta game! Whatta game!"

O

15

Our winning streak didn't last long. For example, until the next game. Detroit beat us, 110–98, in the Garden. We just didn't have it. We left it all in Cleveland. That game with Cincinnati took a lot out of us.

So the streak that started with Detroit ended with Detroit. The Pistons pulled something new. They had Butch Komives play Frazier and run him away from the ball handler. They didn't want Clyde in any position to use his fast hands to steal the ball. Komives worked like a forward and went deep into the corners. Frazier played between him and the ball.

The strategy really wasn't that significant. I think we would have lost, anyway, the way we played. We were flat from start to finish. What made us feel better was the way the Garden fans reacted to the end of our streak. They gave the players a standing ovation as time ran out on the record run. It is hard really to explain the feeling when 19,500 people express their appreciation that way. They had come to expect us to win every game and now they were trying to tell us how sorry they were we finally lost. "At least we're back to being human beings," said Reed when it was over.

The price of fame. People were beginning to recognize me. That's what an eighteen-game winning streak can do. For years, I'd stop in the Turnpike Delicatessen for some sandwiches and the guy behind the counter wouldn't say a thing. Suddenly he began talking basketball. Somebody must have told him who I was. Now I got conversation with my pastrami and corned beef.

It was worse in Cedarhurst. They didn't know me in the Chinese laundry or in the butcher shop. Now they stopped me. I'd notice people whispering. And the kids. They really were something. I remember one day, it was a Sunday, I was home reading the paper. It was early. There was a knock on the door. It was a kid from the neighborhood. He would like an autograph.

I gave it to him. Then I asked how his father would feel if someone came around on Sunday morning, his day off, and disturbed him. I would tell my kid the same thing. He left. Later there was a knock on the door. It was the same kid. This time he had a friend with him. How are you going to beat them?

I am not trying to tell you everyone recognized Red Holzman. Far from it. Some people in the Garden didn't even know me. The game after Detroit broke our streak, we played Seattle and we were coming from our dressing room at half time. The Garden puts ushers and special cops in the area leading onto the floor to keep the crowd from congregating.

Our players came out and they cleared a path for them. I came out a few minutes later and wanted to cut across the court as I always do. But I was stopped by an usher. "Have you got a ticket?" he asked. "No," I said. "You can't go through, then," I was told. Someone rescued me.

We had a new winning streak of one after we beat the

Sonics, 129–109. You could tell the players were glad the old one was over. They were real loose. Tom Meschery said it. "The Knicks are a bunch of guys who all of a sudden realize it's fun to play basketball," said the Poet Laureate of the NBA. "The guys have smiles on their faces as they pass the ball right past your ear."

We were 24-2 and people were saying eloquent things about us. Red Auerbach was moved to comment on the Knicks. "They haven't done it yet, not for one year," he said. "They can go to the end and if Willis Reed gets hurt, what have they won? That's what people want to know, what have you won?"

Auerbach analyzed our team. "Right now, I don't know of any center more valuable than Reed," he said. "He does everything that has to be done. He rebounds. He shoots. He's the leader out there. He's a fantastic athlete. He's a superstar." No argument.

"Frazier is what I call a complete ballplayer," continued Auerbach. "He's a fine passer, not great but real good. He's a wonderful defensive player. He gets people jittery when he's guarding them. They don't have a guy who's going to be blocking shots but they've got a scrambling type of defense and that enhances Frazier." No argument.

Auerbach ran through the team. Dave DeBusschere: "A tower of strength. He makes few mistakes." Bill Bradley: "He was one of the great passers in college and when I said that people didn't believe me. He's proved what I said. He's doing everything." Dick Barnett: "Everyone figured he was the type of guy who would concern himself with what he scored, but he's fit right in." The bench, or the Minutemen as they were called: "They have so many people." No arguments.

We were creating a little excitement, that was for sure. It was great for us and it was good for the other teams when we played in their buildings. We were drawing people and that was good for everyone. It didn't matter to anyone that New York had not finished first in so long. We were on top right now and people came out to see us when we were out of town.

We went to Baltimore, where they didn't exactly like New York from the last picture: the Super Bowl of 1969 and the World Series of 1969. We were the Mets and Jets in Knicks clothing. They greeted us with "Kick the Knick" buttons. Everyone was wearing them. Even some of our players grabbed a few and pinned them on their uniforms in the dressing room. Anything for a laugh.

That was our dressing room. The players spent most of the time kibitzing, opening mail, or listening to soul music coming from Barnett's radio at home or Reed and Bowman's casettes on the road. I preferred it that way. Nothing serious until a few minutes before we went onto the floor. Then we'd run over some things.

They were simple reminders about the other team. No big strategy or last-minute plays. If a team isn't ready by then, it's not going to get ready in the dressing room. I always had a mental picture of the other team and so did the players. But you have a tendency to forget. You can't retain everything when you play as often as we do.

That's where films are invaluable. We do more filming in the Garden than anyone. I like to look at a game film around five in the afternoon so that it remains fresh in my mind. I sometimes take films on the road. You'd be surprised what you can forget or think you remember.

The "Kick the Knick" buttons were funny to the players, but the men were serious when they had to be serious. I could see the fringe benefits of that eighteen-game winning streak in our poise. That final game in Cleveland had taught us no lead was safe, no matter who holds it. We also came out of that stretch with a lot of confidence. Not that we didn't have it before. We did.

We just seemed to have more after we had won so many games. Baltimore got in front by thirteen and looked as though it was going to win easily. But we kept coming. Our bench finally got us going and we actually were in front by six at the half. Cazzie, Stallworth, Bowman and Riordan turned the game for us. We went on to win, 116–107, and we were twenty-five and two. "Their bench brought them back and I was amazed," said Shue. He was amazed but I wasn't.

We beat Milwaukee and it became 26-2. That started a new round of record talk. Philadelphia had gotten off to a 26-2 start in 1966-67 and went on to set an all-time high of sixty-eight wins. It was much too early to dream dreams like that. I borrowed a phrase from some great phrase-maker and kept telling the newspapermen we were just playing them one at a time.

Others were saying other things. "I have never seen a team move the ball like the Knicks . . . hit the open man like the Knicks," said Larry Costello. "The Knicks are playing the best overall basketball I've ever seen," said Guy Rodgers. "I've finally come to the conclusion this is the greatest team I've ever played on," said Walt Frazier. He had to have his little joke.

So did some of the other Knicks. They got into the swing of things because the writers wanted to know. And when writers want to know, there always seems to be someone available to tell them what they want to know.

Hosket said he and May played on a Belmont High School team that was 26-1, so he was not convinced this was the best team he had ever played on, yet. Riordan recalled he played with a pickup team that ran Reed and Emmette Bryant right out of the schoolyard in Bayside. Bradley mentioned his Olympic team of 1965 that had on it the Van Arsdales, Billy Cunningham, Lou Hudson, Joe Ellis and Fred Hetzel.

"Now at Tennessee A&I, we won three NAIA champion-ships in a row," said Barnett. But the topper was Warren. The rookie really set everyone straight. As far as he was concerned, this was the best team for which he had played. "I was four and ten at Far Rockaway High and then two and twelve," he volunteered.

We had a lot of guys on the team with a sense of humor. They were nice and easy because they were winning. I realized that. But they won because they were serious about winning. They had made a lot of sacrifices to get this far. It had taken a lot of blood, sweat and nerves. They had overcome the toughest obstacle—that of getting twelve different personalities to live and play together. They had different tastes, different attitudes and different degrees of patience but they were a team and they were winning.

It reminded me of what Dr. Eric Berne, the psychiatrist who wrote *Games People Play*, said about winning—or losing. "If you're going to play you might as well play to win. Losers spend time explaining why they lost. . . . Losers spend their lives thinking about what they're going to do. They rarely enjoy doing what they're doing as they do it."

Now I don't profess to being a psychiatrist, but we were winning and we were enjoying it and that is what I had set out to accomplish. Everyone can't be a winner. But you have to work to win and play to win if you are in-volved in anything where winning is the ultimate goal.

Why are players and coaches so obsessed with winning? Pride and money, I would say. Pride is the motivation and money is the reward. There are times when pride even overcomes all thought of money, believe it or not.

I think of Bill Bridges, for example. He was terribly upset when the Knicks beat the Hawks by twenty-four points in the Garden and then won by thirty in Atlanta on

Thanksgiving Eve. "In Atlanta, that embarrassed me as a man and a player," he said. "As an athlete, to get beat is one thing. But there's a difference when you're humiliated and have your ego torn apart."

Those people who look on pro basketball as a kid's game just need to get in there a little closer when Bridges and Reed are playing each other—like in between them. They're some battles. They were matched more when we had Bellamy and Willis played forward, but every now and then Guerin switches Bridges to Reed because he has the muscle.

"Last year," said Bridges after Atlanta beat us, 125–124, in overtime in the Garden, "Willis had me clawed on the back, he broke my tooth. Willis is the best player in the league. Every man in this room will say that." Bridges laughed. He could afford to laugh. His team had won and his injured pride had been given a treatment.

We had an anniversary on December 19. It was a year to the day that we got DeBusschere from Detroit. We were 69-21 since the trade and leading the league in just about everything—won and lost, books, magazine articles and cover stories. Someone suggested that the next cover for the Knicks would be the Bible.

We were heading for Chicago with a three-game losing streak. Some newspapermen asked the players if they thought it had been a good trade. They were kidding, of course. They said they had to put some humor in their stories sometimes. "Yeah," said Frazier, "but the way we're going, we may have to pull another trade and send DeBusschere back."

Clyde laughed. "Look what he's done for Bradley," said Frazier, a little more serious. "When Komives was here, he would kid Bill, but Dave treats him like a man. He has helped Bradley to become a good player. He has even taught him how to drink beer." Clyde chuckled at his own humor.

We beat the Bulls, 108–99, for DeBusschere. He helped by playing forty-six minutes and hitting ten of his sixteen shots. So did Reed with twenty-five points and twenty-five rebounds. It was a pleasure to watch those two guys work together. They were the heart of our defense. They had to protect the middle and the basket. They had to protect the boards.

They were perfect team players. When they weren't rebounding, they were boxing out so Bradley or Frazier or Barnett could clear the board. We were not the biggest team by any means. We spotted a lot of size to plenty of teams. We had to make it up by helping out with the rebounds.

Most of the time, we were on the short end in the rebounding statistics because of our size. That is why we worked so hard on our defense. We had to force the other team into tough shots or steal the ball, if we could. That is why any game where we held the other team under one hundred points made us feel good. It is usually very difficult to lose a game like that.

Pretty soon the newspapermen came around and reminded me that I had an anniversary. It was December 27, 1969. Two years earlier I had become the coach of the Knicks. It was something special only to the reporters. I had gotten my present two nights prior to that in the Garden. We had beaten the Pistons with what we call our "one-second play."

We had practiced the play over and over for just such a spot. We would simulate a situation where we would be losing by a point or two with only a second to go and the ball at midcourt. There wasn't enough time to pass-in and then take a shot. So we worked on Frazier throwing

180

a long pass near the hoop and Reed going up and putting it in. It called for perfect timing at both ends.

It is a very difficult play. Frazier had a lot of trouble in practice hanging the pass just right. But that's what practice is all about. We tried it in the overtime game with Atlanta that we lost, but Joe Caldwell spoiled it by deflecting the pass-in. There was nothing else to do when Bellamy drove for a layup and put Detroit ahead, 111–110, with a second to go.

We were lucky to get a time-out at that spot. I really shouldn't say lucky. We were alert enough to call it and get what looked like an impossible shot at winning. We had a second to get the ball in from midcourt and get off a shot. "The one-second play," I advised the players in the huddle. We reviewed our assignments.

It wasn't just a pass from Frazier to Reed. We had to make sure Willis got clear near the hoop so he would be in position to take the pass. We had worked on that in practice. It was Barnett's job to come around a screen and set a pick. Every player had an assignment.

The darn thing worked better than it ever did in practice. Frazier hung the ball about a yard from the basket. Barnett managed his pick. Reed timed the lob pass perfectly and banked it in while in the air. The clock, of course, does not start until the ball touches someone on the court, so there was just enough time for the basket to count.

Our guys went wild. You'd think we had just won the championship. Things like that make all those hours in the gym look good. Frazier played it real cool in the dressing room. "I was trying to make the basket," he said to Reed, sitting right next to him. "I'm glad I spoiled it," answered Willis.

Frazier is quite a passer. He was a quarterback in high school and jokingly refers to himself as the Johnny Unitas of Atlanta. His favorite story concerns the time he quarterbacked his team to the championship. He was fighting the clock and once he was trapped and had to complete a pass with his left hand.

Clyde insists that everyone but he was hysterical. He claims he was on his way into the end zone with the winning touchdown when he ran into the tackle on his own team. "The guy was so upset, he cried," says Frazier. He finally took the team in and his high school won the title. He probably could have been a great quarterback. He has all the qualifications. Let's just say the Knicks are happy he picked basketball.

The last-second victory over Detroit was Christmas night, two days before my so-called anniversary. It will be a long time before I forget that occasion. It fell smack in the middle of a seven thousand-mile trip for three games in three nights. We left New York for Los Angeles on a midnight plane after the game with Detroit. We arrived in Los Angeles at 6:30 A.M., New York time.

We lost that night to the Lakers, 114–106, with West getting forty points and ten assists. The next day, we were up at 6:45 for an 8:30 flight to Vancouver, arriving at 11:15. We beat the Seattle Supersonics, 119–117, and hauled ourselves off for a little sleep—very little.

We climbed out of bed at 5:45 for a six-hour trip to Phoenix by way of Portland, Los Angeles and San Diego. We touched all the bases. That plane must have been a local. We reached our hotel in Phoenix at four in the afternoon and hardly had time to admire our rooms in Del Webb's Towne House. On the bus an hour and fifteen minutes later and to the Veterans Coliseum for a game with the Suns. I think we got fed intravenously.

Everyone was tired. I made up my mind to use the bench as much as possible. I had them on the floor before the first quarter was over. Reed played fourteen minutes and DeBusschere eight in the first half. Dave would have played a little more but he had gotten into foul trouble.

We were losing, 57–52, at the half. The second half was something else. Reed and DeBusschere went wild. Willis had a twenty-point third period. Dave hit four straight shots, giving him eight in a row since he had hit four in a row in the first half before I lifted him. We wound up shooting 72 per cent in the second half (18-for-25) and Johnny Kerr couldn't believe it. I couldn't believe it. We scored eighty-three points in the second half and won, 135–116.

We should've been pooped. We should've been too tired to put on our sneakers. "I remember those train trips from Syracuse to Chicago," recalled Kerr. "We'd get in so tired and then we'd go out so nice and loose, and we'd play great ball." It does work that way sometimes. It is remarkable the way human beings can adjust to things that seem impossible at times.

When we got back to New York, we actually had traveled 7172 miles. Some people don't travel that much in a lifetime. I went home and stayed home. We had an afternoon game with Chicago scheduled for the next day. I even passed up the Holiday Festival that was going on in the Garden.

I'm sure the trip had nothing to do with it, but Willis started to complain about his stomach. He had pain and he thought it might be an ulcer. We called Dr. Yanagisawa into the dressing room one night to examine him. We were taking no chances. Willis and his health were very important to us.

"Nothing serious, just cramps," Yana told Willis, who was stretched out on the trainer's table. "Do you think you'll live, captain?" inquired Frazier. "Yeah," replied Willis, a smile replacing the pain on his face. "If not," said

Clyde, "I'll say a prayer for you. I know the devil has your soul."

We had just lost to Milwaukee and Boston, but we hadn't lost our sense of humor. The Bucks had beaten us for the first time in their two seasons, 118–105, and you could see them growing. They played a harassing defense and Alcindor was just marvelous. He got forty-one points and eighteen rebounds. Bob Dandridge was great. He stole a few balls late in the game that really hurt us.

"It's come, I think so," said Alcindor. "There are other things I know I can do now. I've stopped rushing my shots. We learned a lot the other times we played New York. It was directly after losing to the Knicks by one point." Lew was referring to a game Bradley won, 96–95, with a shot from the corner.

We tried our best to handle Alcindor but he was impossible that night. The Bucks opened it up and managed to isolate Lew on Reed. "They go to him more against us," said Willis. "There's not much I can do. He has such a height advantage on me. They took advantage of all the shots he has—and he has an abundant supply."

Were those Milwaukee fans excited. The Bucks had just made it ten out of eleven and moved into second place behind us. The fans refused to leave the building. They waited for Alcindor to come out of the dressing room for a television show and they mobbed him. He was the biggest thing to hit Milwaukee since Schlitz. The way you spelled Alincdor was t-r-o-u-b-l-e.

We were having a little of our own troubles. Reed's arthritic knees were bothering him for a change. We also were in the process of leveling off after winning eighteen straight. We were 11-8 since the streak ended and everywhere we went, people wanted to know what was wrong. We had spoiled them, I guess. They expected us never to lose.

Truthfully, I never expect to lose, either. Unfortunately, the other coach and his players have the same idea. We were in no panic. It was just a natural letdown. We had lost our sharpness. There was only one prescription—more work. We kept practicing. The players did not like the idea of losing. Who does? They really appreciated how fortunate they were when they went to Baltimore and won by thirty. Now, there's frustration! We had beaten the Bullets for the eighth straight time.

Shue tried something new again. He started LeRoy Ellis on Bradley at forward and put Gus Johnson on Frazier. "We haven't any success against them," explained Gene, "and it's silly to keep doing the same thing. I've got a great sense of humor and great optimism but none of my darn plays work."

That was a pretty tall team Shue started. "Why shouldn't they try something new," said Frazier. "Every game they're experimenting and trying to beat us. I don't mind them changing things but keep that Gus Johnson off me. He's tough to get around." Our defense was sharp, again. We held Baltimore to ninety-nine points and then went to San Francisco and held the Warriors under one hundred. We won 99–94.

Frankie Blauschild informed us it was the twentieth time in our forty-four games we had held the other team under one hundred. Not bad if you like statistics. Much better when you realize we won every time the other team failed to reach one hundred. We were thirty-five and nine at that point and that is what interested us.

We had a few more stops on that road trip. First San Diego and Salt Lake City where we were to play Phoenix. They both had new coaches. Alex Hannum had replaced Jack McMahon in San Diego and general manager Jerry Colangelo had stepped in at Phoenix for Johnny Kerr.

Elvin Hayes showed up for our game with a Yul Brunner cut. The Big E explained his four-year-old son had dug a divot in his head so he shaved off all his hair. Hannum walked into the dressing room and spotted Hayes's bare head. Alex rubbed his own. "I'll deck the first guy who says a word," he warned his players.

The Rockets laughed. They were nice and loose. Too loose. They beat us, 123–115. The Big E was happy as a kid. "A lot of people said I was a spoiled kid," he said. "You got to make basketball fun. Hannum's made it that way." I was sorry for McMahon but happy for Alex. He had contributed a lot of excitement to the NBA before he left for a job in the ABA and now he was back.

We went to Salt Lake City where Colangelo played Connie Hawkins on Barnett. We won, 130–114, but we were concerned about Reed. His stomach again. We moved on to Detroit and decided to have Willis undergo an ulcer test as soon as possible. He wanted to see a doctor. He wanted to take the GI series.

"It hurts when I play," he told me and Danny Whelan. "Some nights it's worse than others. It doesn't stop." He agreed to wait for an examination until the next convenient open date. We were playing in Detroit on Friday and Boston on Sunday, so the exam would be in New York the following Monday.

Meanwhile, he would stay with us in Detroit, or Windsor, Canada. We had to check into the Holiday Inn across the river because salesmen conventions had taken all the rooms in Detroit. That meant we had to travel back and forth through customs to practice in Cobo Hall.

Each day we faced possible inspection. Sometimes it was only a spot check. Other times they let our bus roll through. Once they asked us all to get off and bring our bags into the building. We were going from Windsor to Detroit on this trip and carrying only equipment bags.

The customs official went through every bag. He peeked

under socks and jocks and sneakers and trunks. He went through ten bags. DeBusschere had gone home to Detroit and Hosket had been given permission to attend to some business in Columbus. They were to meet us at practice.

When the inspector got the last bag, he moved it over to Frazier. "Are you a team or something?" the guy asked. "Sometimes," said Clyde. That was on our first day of practice. The second day was a real beauty. It had nothing to do with customs.

Cazzie had driven over to Michigan University in the morning. He made practice by about five minutes and came back with some story. There was a huge manhunt on for a guy by the name of A. J. Simpson at the time. The papers were full of A. J. Simpson and how he allegedly killed a sheriff who was escorting him to prison.

Well, Cazzie, it seems, ran into a roadblock on his way back from the university. "I borrowed a car from Fred Snowden," explained Cazzie, speaking of John Orr's assistant at Michigan. "I was driving along the highway and I saw these cops and they were signaling everyone to stop. One came over and asked for my license and registration."

Cazzie reached into the glove compartment for Snowden's registration. He was ordered out of the car. He wanted to know why. He was told to get out of the car. He got out. He didn't realize it but the police probably figured he was going for a gun in the glove compartment.

One policeman talked and when Cazzie glanced over his shoulder he saw another draped over the hood of the car with a gun aimed at him. Caz still didn't understand. Again he asked why. They told him. "Someone in your race committed a murder," the policeman said. "He had a slight mustache and he was 6-3½ or 6-4."

Now there was a coincidence. Cazzie had a slight mustache and he was 6-5. The one policeman finally looked at the registration and the license. Caz explained about the registration. "I'm sorry, Cazzie," the officer finally said. "I'm just doing my job. There's been a murder. A prisoner was being escorted to Jackson and he killed a deputy sheriff."

Cazzie confessed he was scared. Why? "I kept looking at my clock," he said. "I didn't want to be late for practice. I didn't want to get fined." Caz was on time—for practice and in the game the next night. He saved it for us with two clutch shots when DeBusschere came up with a cramp.

I had to take DeBusschere out with 2:22 to go. We were leading by only 94–92. Cazzie hit twice as soon as he came in to give us a cushion and we went on to win, 104–102. Reed, bad stomach and all, had quite a game. He scored twenty-nine points, blocked eight shots and had fourteen rebounds. Now I realize the trouble with my game when I played was that I never had a bad stomach.

We lost in Boston and Willis went back to New York for his ulcer examination. No ulcer. It was just a nervous stomach. Nothing serious. He could play in the all-star game in Philadelphia. I was glad. I would hate to coach any team without Willis Reed and I was coaching the East against the West. I would hate to play any game without him.

I remember one night in San Diego. He had come into the dressing room complaining he wasn't feeling well. I suggested maybe he shouldn't play. I was only kidding but he took it seriously. He agreed. "Maybe, you oughta just try it and see what happens," I said, quickly changing my approach. "Okay, Red, whatever you say," he answered.

He must have been sick. Not because we lost. That can happen anytime. But when Willis does not feel like playing, there must be something seriously wrong with him. He has had more than his share of aches, bruises and broken bones, but he always is ready. He would play if you had to wheel him out there. We almost did one night. That's another story.

O

16

Willis Reed, Lew Alcindor, Oscar Robertson, John Havlicek, Billy Cunningham, Walt Frazier, Gus Johnson, Hal Greer, Dave DeBusschere, Jim Walker, Tom Van Arsdale and Flynn Robinson. How do they expect a coach to win with material like that?

It was tough. But the East beat the West, 142–135, and Reed was voted the Most Valuable Player and I am thankful I didn't mess it up. It was Willis's first trophy since he came into the NBA and a better man never deserved it more.

We on the Knicks had a few other things on our mind. They voted expansion the day before the game. Buffalo, Cleveland, Portland and Houston were granted franchises. Houston was to drop out. But it meant anxiety for some players on our team at a time when everyone was involved in trying to win a championship.

We had been through it before and Eddie Donovan and I remembered so well how unpleasant it turned out to be for Dick Van Arsdale and Emmette Bryant. Now we had to worry about losing three more players at the end of the season. More importantly, the players were sure to worry about it.

It was not an ideal situation. You don't have to tell that to certain players who are vulnerable in expansion. When you are allowed to protect only seven and the others go into a pool, it is very easy to figure. You work so hard to get players to feel they are part of a team and then suddenly some of them can see where they will not be around another season.

But that's progress. The NBA has come a long way in recent years. It has expanded all over the country and brought pro basketball to many people who had never seen it before. It has stimulated greater interest by spreading from the East and Midwest to Los Angeles, San Francisco, San Diego, Seattle, Portland, Phoenix and Atlanta.

Players do understand they can be moved to another team at any time. But a coach never really knows what effect an announcement about expansion has on certain players—especially those who are getting little playing time. All we could do was hope that it would be no serious distraction. We had to have everyone dedicated to what the Knicks were or there could be trouble.

Fortunately, we had the type of player who apparently felt the only important thing was to win, no matter what uniform he wore. Hosket, for instance. He came down with the flu right at all-star time. He was sick at home when we got news that DeBusschere's back was bothering him.

Dave figured it happened during the all-star game. Just to make it a little worse, he was driving home on the Long Island Expressway and got a flat. He fixed it himself, bad back and all. That put him out of our game in Chicago, one in the Garden with San Diego and another in Boston.

You can imagine how Hosket felt. No DeBusschere meant he would have gotten some playing time. He couldn't take it any longer after the first two games. He called us in Boston and told us he was grabbing a morning plane. He was weak but he couldn't stand missing the opportunity.

"What a time to be home sick," Hosket said to Frazier. He got sympathy from Clyde. "Yeah, Hos," said Frazier. "I heard the neighbors called the cops because you were stomping on the floor and kicking over chairs." We won our third straight without DeBusschere and Hosket played seven minutes.

It was a mini-streak. We won in Chicago on Friday night and flew right home, getting to bed around three in the morning. We won at home Saturday night and flew to Boston after the game and won there Sunday afternoon. Everything was fine. Stallworth had his periodic checkup and came back with a good report. We were streaking, again.

Bradley twisted an ankle and couldn't play but we moved Cazzie up and we kept winning. The worst of it for Bill, I assume, was that he had to sit next to me on the bench. It was tranquil for the most part until we went to Philadelphia for a game. Every game down there is exciting but this one had something extra.

We had won five in a row and it looked like six pretty easily when we put it together in the third period. For some reason, it seemed to keep happening in the third period for us. The 76ers were leading, 50–49, and wham, just like that, we were in front, 90–72. We only blew five of nineteen shots in one span. Cazzie, Frazier and Barnett couldn't miss.

It wasn't over. The 76ers never let you get away that easily. They spurted back and pretty soon they were climbing our backs. So were a couple of guys behind our bench. I was trying to concentrate on the game but I could hear these guys snarling at each other.

192

I sneaked a peek. There was this one guy in the front row telling a couple of guys behind him to watch their beer. I guess it was dripping on him. Then it happened. I heard this rumble behind me. I turned and they were coming right at the bench. They were swinging. We jumped up and tried to clear out, but they were in among us before we could get away.

The bench went over. People went down. The press table went down. I don't know how I escaped but I did. DeBusschere came running over to see if I was alright. "I thought it was you," said Dave, "but when it wasn't anyone I knew, I went away."

All the Knicks played it smart. They got far away from the action. Frazier sat under the basket and watched the guys swinging at each other. "I didn't want to get hit by any stray punches," said Clyde. "If that fight started spreading, I was going to send the captain over to break it up."

Willis wanted no part of it. "There was hell going on over there," said Reed. "Those guys meant business. I wasn't going over. That was no basketball fight. Somebody breaks ours up after one punch. Those guys were really swinging."

And how! While they were swinging, one guy's coat opened and he had a gun. It turned out he was a transit patrolman from New York. He and another transit police-man had come down to root for the Knicks and, in their excitement, began spilling their beer on the guy in front. That's how the fight started. It ended with the transit policemen being escorted from the Spectrum.

We won in Philadelphia and we headed for Detroit. The trading dealine was on us. It was midnight, February 1. We had no deals in mind. We were very well satis-fied with our players.

We beat the Pistons and immediately after the game

they announced a trade. They were sending Walt Bellamy to Atlanta for money and a player to be named. They were trading Eddie Miles and a fourth-draft pick to Baltimore for Bob Quick and a second-draft choice.

There was more. Cincinnati had arranged a deal with Baltimore for Oscar Robertson but the Big O turned it down. He had a clause in his contract that gave him the right of refusal. The newspapermen asked if we were interested in Oscar. That was Donovan's territory as general manager.

"Well, let's just say we are glad he didn't wind up in Baltimore," Eddie told the reporters. A nice, diplomatic answer, I'd say. I'll have to remember that when someone asks the present general manager of the Knicks a question like that.

I know this. For years Donovan brought up Oscar's name whenever he talked to Cincinnati. How do I know? He said so. "At the beginning, we really worked hard to get Oscar," Eddie explained. "It's understandable why we couldn't get him. I don't think he ever was available and rightly so. We would talk about Oscar and Jerry Lucas. But I don't think it ever was serious on Cincy's part. Oscar was what we needed badly. He was a leader. A great talent."

Time had changed our situation and who would want to fool around with a team that was forty-six and eleven? "Off the way we're going, I would say the backcourt is no problem," said Donovan. "Oscar's just a fantastic player, but Frazier has come along and things have changed."

They sure had. For a lot of people. When we got to Atlanta, we had won nine straight and Bellamy was wearing his new uniform. The Hawks were jubilant and had every right to be. They were getting just what they needed—an experienced center.

"This is the start of a new season for us," said Walt

Hazzard. Not that Atlanta was doing so badly. It was in first place in the West. But Bells represented a lot more to the Hawks. They really were excited about getting him.

The first thing we saw when we checked into the Marriott Hotel in Atlanta was Bill Bridges sitting in the restaurant. The same Bridges who has all that pride I told you about. Bellamy had moved into the hotel and Bill had come right over to see him.

"I'm the captain of the team and he is my responsibility" explained Bill. "Hotel rooms can be kind of cold, especially if you've just been traded. I came over to talk to him. I think he's found his first real home with us. He's needed here. Ever since I've been a Hawk, we've never had that monster in the middle. He'll get plenty of attention here—from me."

We lost that night. Bellamy played only twenty minutes because he needed time to adjust, but he hit five of his nine shots and grabbed twelve rebounds. Guerin once used a front line of Bellamy, Bridges and Jim Davis. Some height! Some game! The only thing I care to remember was something that happened in the third period.

A mouse ran up the floor. Yes, a mouse. He didn't even report to the scorer's table. The sight of that mouse and the size of the players on the floor brought a funny thing to mind. Don't ask me why, but I said to myself: "Whatever became of the small man in basketball?"

We had to make a decision around that time on Phil Jackson. His back was getting better and he was running around and shooting baskets and playing a little one-on-one, but he wasn't ready to go all out. The doctor advised us not to let him play. There was no sense rushing him and taking the calculated risk of having him hurt himself. So Jackson was out for the season and out of the playoffs.

Bradley hurt his ankle again and once more he didn't play in Philadelphia. He stayed in New York for treatment.

"It's a shame Bradley had to stay home," said Billy Cunningham after Cazzie hit from every conceivable angle. At one time, Caz and Barnett had thirty-nine points between them or more than the 76ers.

All Caz did was score thirty-five points and we won by forty-five. There is nothing a coach can do about that. Our bench alone accounted for forty-seven points. I hear people complain that teams pile it on. There is no way you can control it in pro basketball. For one thing, there is the twenty-four-second clock and a team must take a shot at the basket. For another, when you have guys sitting and then put them in the game, they are just too hungry for points.

I can assure you any coach who has a team that wins, 151–106, like we did against the 76ers, feels sorry for the other coach and his team. It is embarrassing all around. But it happens to everyone at some time or another. What are you going to do? "I'm going home and watch the Johnny Carson show," was the suggestion of Cunningham.

Just to show you how those things work out, we were lucky to beat the 76ers by two points the next night in the Garden. We knew it would happen. "We should've saved some of those points for tomorrow night," said Donnie May after that Philadelphia rout. Darrall Imhoff also knew it. "I'll bet it doesn't happen again tomorrow night," said the 76er center.

The final score was, 116–114. A funny thing happened on our way to that victory. It was late in the game and we were leading by two. They called a foul on Cunningham and he got upset. He walked over to our bench to plead his case. Of all people he picked out DeBusschere. I had just taken Dave out because he had gotten his fifth personal.

"Would you believe that?" Billy said to DeBusschere. "What're you looking to me for sympathy for?" answered

Dave, laughing. "He just called the fifth on me." Cunningham walked away muttering to himself. I wonder if he got sympathy elsewhere?

We were fiifty-one and thirteen with eighteen games to go. Milwaukee was second with forty-five and twenty and seventeen games remaining. The newspapermen began playing their favorite little game of magic numbers. This is how it works: Milwaukee had seventeen games to play and if it won them all, the most it could wind up with would be sixty-two victories. That meant if we won only twelve of our remaining eighteen games, we would have sixty-three victories and could not lose first place. Thus our magic number was twelve.

It's simple arithmetic. It's simple on paper. It's a lot tougher when you have to play the games. Even when we concentrated on basketball, and played our best, Atlanta came into the Garden and beat us again. Then we went down to Baltimore and the Bullets finally beat us. They felt good about it. We felt horrible.

I should have suspected they were going to gang up on us. Johnny Unitas showed up. So did Frank Robinson. The Knicks might have been better off if those two had played instead of Earl Monroe and Wes Unseld or Gus Johnson. The doctor had advised Johnson to rest a pulled stomach muscle, but he insisted on playing. Gus must have known something.

They did the job on us. They won, 110–104, but we scared them for a while. They got in front by fourteen and then we went ahead by two. Frazier got sixteen of his thirty points in the third period alone. They weren't enough. Baltimore outscored us, 36–22, in the final quarter.

The Bullets were happy. They had lost nine in a row to the Knicks and people down in Baltimore were talking about a New York complex. "We promise to show up at all the Mets and Jets games from now on," said Kevin

Loughery after Baltimore had won. "I can't tell you how pleased I am today," said Gene Shue. "That streak was very difficult. We had to get off the schneid before the playoffs. Give everyone a beer."

The playoffs weren't that far off, come to think of it. Only fifteen more games to the end of the season for us. What was next? Bad news. Dr. Yanagisawa died. He had been the Garden doctor for I don't know how many years. A fine guy. He treated the Rangers and Knicks like his sons. The players respected him.

Emmette Bryant, for example, flew in from Boston for the funeral. Em had a game that night but he came down anyway. He remembered how Yana had operated on his torn knee cartilage. He figured he would pay his respects and get back to Boston in time for the game.

We all met at the Thirty-third Street employees' entrance to the Garden. We had three limousines and one private car. There were thirteen Knicks, including Phil Jackson, and Donovan, me, Dick McGuire, Alvin Cooperman, executive vice-president of the Garden, Danny Whelan, Jimmy Wergeles and a newspaperman.

Tom Hoover, who used to play for the Knicks, was driving the private car. Bryant, Nate Bowman and Dave Stallworth piled in with Hoover. The others went in the limousines. We left the Garden for Bergenfield, New Jersey, around 11:45 for the one o'clock services. I would guess we arrived at the funeral parlor around 12:30. There was a message to call the Garden. It was urgent.

Donovan called. He came back. He told Alvin Cooperman and me there was trouble. Stallworth, Hoover and Bryant had been arrested. They were in the police station. We had to get back as soon as we could. We got all the details when we got to the station house later.

We went back to the Garden first. Donovan called the police station and was told by the lieutenant it was alright to come over. We went upstairs to a small room that had a table and some chairs. Hoover, Bryant and Stallworth were there. So was Bernie Fliegal. He's an attorney. We both played ball at City College. Hoover had called and asked him to come over.

I looked at Stallworth, Bryant and Hoover. "What are you guys doing here?" I said. Pretty clever. What else could I say? They were sitting in chairs. They looked pretty sad. The lieutenant said they had been picked up with a stolen car. He had to check out the story. Meanwhile, Donovan and I pieced it together with the help of the players.

When the three limousines left the Garden, the private car, driven by Hoover, made a stop at the Hotel New Yorker around the corner. Stallworth wanted to drive his car. Bowman had borrowed it that morning and put it in the hotel garage but left the ticket in his room. Nate got out and the others waited in front of the hotel. Along came a patrol car. It stopped when it spotted last year's blue inspection ticket on the windshield of Hoover's car. The proper one was green.

By the time Bowman got back to the car, Hoover, Bryant and Stallworth were being questioned. The police had asked for Hoover's license and he produced it. They asked for the registration but Tom couldn't produce it. He explained that he had borrowed the car from a friend.

They were taken down the street to the precinct on Thirty-fifth Street near Ninth Avenue. They couldn't figure why they were being hauled in simply because Hoover didn't have a registration. They found out when they got to the station house that the car had been stolen on April 2 of the previous year—almost eleven months ago.

We had to wait until the police brought in the friend who had loaned the car to Hoover. The story checked out and the three of them were released. "Victims of circumstances," said Stallworth, playing it cool. "I come down from Boston for a funeral and wind up in jail," said Bryant.

Emmette was worried about Red Auerbach and missing the game. Donovan informed Em he had called Red and told him the story. "The only thing I'm sorry about is that I missed the funeral," said Bryant. It had been an ordeal. They had been in custody for about five hours.

Bowman was lucky. He escaped because he had gone into the hotel for the ticket to Stallworth's car. Hoover was relieved because he had borrowed the hot car. They all were tired.

"Who's going to drive me home?" Bryant asked. He was living in New York, where his wife, Barbara, teaches, and residing in Boston during the basketball season. "You want to ride with me?" volunteered Hoover.

O

17

Practice was over at Lost Battalion Hall in Rego Park. I checked out the players and talked to Danny Whelan a while about Bill Bradley's ankle that still was bothering him.

Bradley had missed twelve games and we wanted him back sometime during our remaining thirteen games but we weren't going to rush him. We decided to let him keep running and have him rejoin us when we made our final swing to the Coast. I went out to pick up my car that I had parked in an alley alongside the building.

The door was open. I climbed in and found the ignition switch broken. Someone had tried to steal it. He apparently used a wire hanger to yank the door handle but probably was frightened away when he saw someone coming. The car wasn't much. It was a small convertible. But it had sentimental value. I had made all the payments.

Lost Battalion Hall was right where Reed and Russell had apartments. They had made an impact on the neighborhood delicatessen. There was a Knicks color poster plastered on the window because of them. Willis and

Cazzie found it very convenient for us to practice so close to their places.

Especially Cazzie, as he demonstrated with a joke one day. We have this rule that when practice is at ten o'clock, everyone has to be on the court and ready by then. No wandering in at ten or a minute or two after. I had been trying to nail Caz for a long time. He knew it. It had become a contest.

He would time it so he would get on the court right under the gun. Well, this one day, he comes rushing into Lost Battalion at five to ten. He had his coat on. "I've got you now, Cazzie," I chuckled. He broke up. He took off his coat. He had his uniform on. The sonofagun had dressed at home, and had his fun.

It wasn't all laughs. We received another jolt when Eddie Donovan advised management he was leaving immediately to become general manager of the new Buffalo franchise. I said it then and I'll say it now: He's a good friend and one of the finest persons I've ever known. I learned a lot from him. I am grateful for what he did for me and that was a great deal.

They asked me to become general manager. I had worked so close with Donovan, I had no apprehension about being able to handle both jobs. He had left a competent staff—secretary Cathy Aspland, Frankie Blauschild and Jimmy Wergeles, and their secretaries, Joanne Dinoia and Gwynne Bloomfield.

Eddie was funny his last day in the office. I knew how he felt about leaving the Knicks. You can't be associated so long with people without creating an emotional attachment. He was fumbling and stumbling as he cleaned out his desk. I suggested he empty all his pockets before he left. "I've gotta get out of here before your press conference, but where will I go?" he said.

Donovan was in Buffalo when we played our next game

the following night. He was not in the Garden to see the team he helped build beat Seattle, 117–99, and clinch a tie for its first Eastern Division crown in sixteen years. But he sent a telegram and I read it to the players before the game.

"Best of luck tonight and every night from here on," the wire read. "Hoping and praying that the best bunch of guys I know will go all the way. Eddie Donovan." It's a shame he had to leave when he did and wasn't there when it finally happened.

We left for Portland the day after the game with Seattle to play the Sonics there. Everyone was talking champagne. Not me. I really didn't want to hear it. I couldn't get worked up about popping corks. It was all presumptuous. We hadn't won anything yet.

Suppose we did clinch first place. What had we accomplished? We still had a long way to go in the playoffs. I didn't want the players thinking the job was finished after eighty-two games. They had worked so hard to get this far and the championship was the big thing. It would be criminal if they were distracted by champagne.

Still the newspapermen kept bugging me about whether we had the champagne ready in case we won in Portland. The Garden arranged to have the game televised back home. They felt the New York fans were entitled to be in on the clinching, the way they had supported the team all season. They even arranged for a camera to be in the dressing room should we do it against the Sonics.

I told the TV people to keep the camera hidden until it happened. I told Whelan to get some champagne but to keep that hidden. I didn't want the Seattle players to see all the fuss. I know how our players would feel if another team had the audacity to arrange for a victory celebration at their expense. We thought we did a good job of keeping everything at a low pitch. We tried, anyway.

Someone must have spotted the champagne and told Lennie Wilkens about it. "Lennie told us they brought the champagne tonight," said Bob Boozer after we were beaten, 115–103. Seattle played inspired ball. It was still fighting for a playoff spot and that might have helped.

We left the unopened champagne in the arena where Whelan had hidden it. An hour or so after we went to our motel, which was within walking distance, Frankie Blauschild had to go back to the arena. He had lost his coat and wanted to see if the maintenance men had it. He found them getting looped on our champagne. They were holding their own victory party.

We made it the next night in San Diego. We beat the Rockets, 106–101, and Bradley finally got into a game. He played only five minutes but he was back. He now had a chance to get ready for the playoffs. We knew by then we would be playing the third place team, which turned out to be the Baltimore Bullets.

Clinching it in San Diego was sort of an anticlimax for the players. They were completely casual when they came into the dressing room. Frazier was one of the first in. "Where's the coke?" he asked. "How about champagne, Red?" said Reed, smiling as though he really didn't mean it. I told him we left it in Portland. There was no champagne. There were no TV cameras.

No one was excited. You would think they had been through all this so many times. They sipped their cokes and some had the beer we brought in. Otherwise they chatted about the division championship and tried to explain their feelings to the newspapermen. "It was the wildest victory celebration since VJ day in Tokyo," was the reaction of Bob Harding of the *Newark Star-Ledger*.

We still had six games to go in the regular season and then the playoffs, so I guess the players accepted the clinching as just part of the whole experience. Or maybe they expected to win so it came as no surprise to them. It was good that they took it in their stride. We left right after the game to catch a plane to Los Angeles.

They ran into a problem. It had something to do with a flat tire, or they couldn't get a crew. Some of the guys wandered off for a beer. DeBusschere bought a round for May and Phil Jackson, who had come along on the trip and brought his camera. Dave told the bartender to have a drink on him.

The bartender wanted to know why. Dave told him the boys were celebrating because they had just won a division championship. "Everyone expected that," said the bartender. It was nice to find out after seventy-six games that it was supposed to be so simple.

We sat in the airport about two hours before we decided to try and get our rooms back for the night. The players were getting restless and tired. Cazzie and Stalls tried to keep them awake by staging a race in wheelchairs. We flew up to Los Angeles the next morning and got some fresh news about Chamberlain.

Just as he had predicted: Wilt was coming back. He showed up at our game that night in the Forum and revealed he would play in a few days and would be ready to help the Lakers in the playoffs. "I'm not surprised at all that I'm back," Wilt said. Neither was I. He was determined to make it and that was good enough for me. When Wilt makes up his mind to do something, he has the inner strength to make sacrifices and apply himself.

"It took a lot of hard work," he said. "I guess you have to be selfish about yourself. The biggest thing was lifting weights, but I've been doing that all my life so that was not torture to me." Nobody knew how much Wilt could play or how much he could help. Everyone knew if he was in uniform, he would contribute. He wouldn't put on the uniform if he didn't think he could.

We talked about our game with Los Angeles and all remaining games that had an effect on the standings. It wouldn't be fair to anyone involved in the struggle for playoff positions to go through the motions. Los Angeles and Atlanta were fighting for first place, for example. "I hope they're that mean against Atlanta," Jerry West said about the Knicks after his thirty-eight points were a major reason we lost, 106–101.

I was more concerned with Bradley. He had played five minutes in San Diego and twelve in Los Angeles. He had to get more playing time. He said his ankle was feeling much better and he could go as much as I wanted to use him. He played thirty-four minutes in our next game in Detroit and came out of it fine.

I planned to ease off on DeBusschere and Reed and give them a blow here and there. They needed it more than anyone by the very nature of the way they play. They took most of the pounding under the boards and they averaged close to forty minutes a game. Frazier came up with a slight groin pull that was not serious but we weren't taking any chances with him.

Fortunately the only remaining game with any playoff significance was in Atlanta. Our games with Detroit and Milwaukee and the finale with Boston had no bearing on the standings. Detroit did have some meaning for Reed. That is where he got the news on our arrival from Los Angeles that he had been voted the Most Valuable Player by the NBA players.

We kept Frazier out of the games with Milwaukee and Atlanta to give him time to heal. DeBusschere worked only six minutes against the Bucks. "I couldn't lift my arms when I was warming up," Dave said. He was mentally and physically exhausted.

DeBusschere is the kind of player who plays himself into exhaustion. Some men know how to pace themselves.

Dave knows no other way than putting his head through the wall all the time he is out there.

There were many games he had to come out because he ran himself into leg cramps, partly because he plays so intensively, partly because he pushes himself beyond the brink of tiredness. I remember the night of our victory party. It was the first time since we had gone to training camp on September 11 that we all truly had a chance to relax. The players and their wives, the Garden people and the news media were there to sit and drink and laugh together.

I believe it was five o'clock in the morning, after the party, the phone rang at home. It was Mrs. DeBusschere. She was upset. She said Dave was ill. She said he had pains in his chest. He thought he was having a heart attack. He had gone to the hospital.

I told Geri I would contact our doctor and have him see Dave as soon as possible. It was no heart attack. It was pure exhaustion. Physical and emotional exhaustion. That's another thing people find hard to understand—that athletes are humans. They yell, cry, argue and hurt like anyone else. People are people. And that goes for coaches and general managers and even guys in the business of writing and broadcasting.

Bradley got another good workout in Detroit. He was in there for thirty-six mintues and you could see the timing coming back. We did not want to lose to Milwaukee in New York but we did under the circumstances. The young Bucks felt good about that because they were heading into their first playoffs against the 76ers. "I know we can win it all but I don't know if we will," said Lew Alcindor. "The Knicks can and the 76ers can."

Down in Atlanta it was a great night. The Hawks beat us to clinch the Western Division title and it was Bill Bridges Night. The whole Bridges family was there.

His mother came in from New Mexico to join Bill, his wife and three kids. He stood in the middle of the floor and the fans gave him a tremendous ovation.

"I never thought it would happen in Atlanta," said Bridges. "I thought I'd never see it. It brought tears to my eyes."

Bridges got a lot of gifts but the one that impressed me most was an expensive sports car. It was from Ben Kerner. That man is something. He never forgets. That car was worth a few thousand dollars, but it wasn't the money. It was the thought—the sincerity.

Sincerity. A very important word. I would guess most people look for that in other people. I know this, there must be a lot of people who think I'm pulling their leg when I talk to them. Yes, I kid around with our players and it's pretty obvious what I'm doing. Like planting room keys in Frazier's pockets and when he finds them, telling him: "You're my key man." And as a change of pace, putting a few in Bradley's bag. Just for laughs.

Who could take that seriously? It's really kid stuff but I think the coach should be involved with his players in some way, and kibitzing once in a while is my way. It is a means of communication in one respect. In the case of Bowman, for example, I think it helped him feel he was wanted after his experiences with other teams.

Bowman gave us maximum mileage. He was an important part of our team. He was the backup for Reed and he helped us in plenty of games. He produced, otherwise someone else would have played. Yet there might be a lot of people who would not understand why I spent so much time keeping Nate involved.

People will believe what they want to believe no matter what you say. I can tell by the way the newspapermen keep asking me about my coaching philosophy. I don't know why that is so important. I've tried to express myself on the subject many times but no one seems to think I'm sincere. Why would they keep asking if they did? I assure you I was not deceiving Seymour Smith, assistant sports editor of the *Baltimore Sun,* when I told him:

"You do your best; you win, you win. You lose, you lose. What are you going to do? You try things the next time but you're not going to help anybody by worrying or letting the pressure get to you.

"When I took this job, I told myself I wasn't going to let it get me the way it did the first time when I coached in St. Louis. I was younger then. I let the pressure get me, pressure that I had built up myself. I would have been content to stay a scout or remain in basketball in some other job.

"I'm past the point where I have to make an image for myself. Look, I'm an average guy. There's nothing special about me. There are people on my block who don't even know who I am, and that's the way I like it. It's just as ridiculous calling me the greatest coach in the game as calling my team that. What have we proved?

"As far as I'm concerned, our won-and-lost record doesn't mean that much. When the playoffs end, then we'll know about this team. You know what makes a successful coach? Lots of hard work and being fortunate enough to have good players. You don't have time, however, to enjoy your records. Maybe if I had ten days off between games, I could enjoy it."

Coaching carries greater responsibility within the framework of pro sports these days. The Garden has a tremendous investment in the Knicks and there is tremendous public interest. A guy like me is hired to get the most out of the personnel and does the best he can within the scope of his knowledge and experience. You borrow from your own experiences and knowledge and from others. There are no new plays or defenses. It's just a matter of how well the players know and execute them. That's why I believe in repetition until it comes out of everyone's ears—including mine.

I will listen to all suggestions from the players. I encourage suggestions. It was the same way when I played. If I felt there was something that would help the team, I would suggest it to Nat Holman or Les Harrison. That's what a coach is all about. He really is the one who should filter all ideas and then decide which are best.

What is to gain by being stubborn and rejecting an idea just because it belongs to somebody else. If it's good, it's good. Take Dave DeBusschere. He came to us from Detroit and was a very important part of our team. He had been a player and a coach. He had an excellent idea as to what plays worked best for him and us. We talked about it and put some in.

I don't have to feed my ego and insist on using only the things I think of. There is no one who knows it all. Somebody came up with the Ted Williams shift and other guys used it because it worked. Somebody came up with the T-formation and other guys used it because it worked. Bill Russell proved the value of a big man who can block shots, now everyone is looking for one.

It is a sign of strength, not weakness, for a coach to recognize what is good for his team and use it from no matter where it comes. I remember the football Giants once won a big game because Allie Sherman used a play suggested by Pete Previtte, the clubhouse man. If a player on our team has a suggestion, I not only want to hear it but I will use it. It is up to me to separate the good from the bad.

That's how I approach the job. Others do it differently. A coach is a coach is a coach. You laugh like anybody else. You yell like anybody else. A guy has to be a fool to think he can please all the people or even all his players. I am

210

sure there are things I have said and done that some players disagree with, just as there are things they have said and done I disagree with. It's all in the eyes of the beholder. It's like two guys watching the same fight and coming up with a different winner.

The important thing is getting the players and the coach to pull in the same direction. This has its difficulties and that is why a coach has to be firm about his convictions and make hard decisions when the time comes, whether the players like it or not. Would it surprise you, for example, if I said I raised my voice to Reed or Bradley or my wife? Would it surprise you if I said our players at times got angry at me or each other? If it does, there's something wrong with you.

We did our share of family growling and I confess I worked at keeping it in the clubhouse and out of the papers. It had a chance of dying a natural death that way. Routine griping is healthy and only damaging when allowed to fester and grow, and people stop talking to each other. Taken out of context, normal differences can be portrayed as being serious by people who do not have the patience or desire to try to understand.

Part of my responsibility as a coach and person is to protect the players and, therefore, the welfare of the team. They are the team and they can make it or break it by how they conduct their business. It is up to me, as coach, to guide and lead them down the right streets—to the best of my ability.

That is why I feel obligated to make players understand the value of keeping certain things in the clubhouse. I know only one way: if you don't have something nice to say, say nothing. I don't believe in knocking because it is destructive. I believe in constructive criticism and, on a ball club, it has the best chance of being constructive if outsiders do not get involved and distort things.

If I tell the players not to discuss fines outside the clubhouse or family, it is to spare them embarrassment. If I tell them to keep their differences to themselves, it is to spare them from having things blown out of proportion. It is basically for their good. If I benefit, then we're all profiting. That's what I consider constructive. That's what I call teamwork.

I knew a baseball manager who couldn't figure how everything leaked from his clubhouse a few minutes after it happened. Every time he fined a player, the newspapermen had it right away. He solved the problem very simply. He called a meeting and told the players the next time it happened, he would announce all fines to the press. If a player came strolling in at four or five in the morning and got fined, the press would have the whole story and the player then would have to explain to his wife. The leaks stopped.

O

18

This is what it is all about in sports. The regular season is the long, exhausting walk to the playoffs or the World Series or the Super Bowl or the Stanley Cup. We had finished with the best record in the NBA but we felt we still had not accomplished anything because only the champion is considered the best.

Baltimore knew what it meant. The Bullets had dominated the East and finished with the best won-and-lost record in the NBA the year before. But the Knicks beat them four straight in the first round, so what did it all mean to Baltimore? It went home feeling as though the whole season was wasted and that was our concern as we faced the playoffs.

We were Baltimore this time and the Bullets were New York. We had the best record in the league and they were coming in to meet us in the first round. We weren't kidding ourselves that the Bullets would be easy just because we had beaten them five times in six games. The playoffs are the start of a new season.

Both teams had their problems. Kevin Loughery started the series wearing a heavy, leather brace. He had run into

Lew Alcindor about a month before the season ended and wound up with four cracked ribs and a punctured lung. Strange about Baltimore. It seems every time the Bullets make the playoffs, someone is badly hurt.

Loughery and Gus Johnson, particularly. Kev had been injured but managed to make the two previous playoffs because he was capable of walking. Not Johnson. He played one game during the 1965-66 playoffs and missed it all when we eliminated Baltimore in four games in 1968-69. Come to think of it, the Knicks had similar problems in the playoffs we made after I became coach.

Walt Frazier got hurt in the 1967-68 series with Philadelphia and never finished. He was hurt the next season when we played Boston the final game. This time it was Willis Reed. His knee was bothering him. He had the occupational disease of most basketball players—an arthritic knee. There was nothing you could do about it but ease the discomfort.

We made no special preparations for the Bullets. They knew us and we knew them. We just went over our own defenses and put in a variation or two on offense. Repetition. I believe in it. Practice makes perfect or something like that. If it doesn't make things perfect, it at least makes a team sharper.

My only concern was that we got off. We had to be sharp right away because Baltimore is not the kind of team you like to chase. Monroe, Unseld, Johnson, Marin and Loughery are too much under ordinary conditions. They are murder out in front.

This is no reflection on any other team, but the Bullets give our defense an awful lot of pressure the way they can shoot. There is no way you can handle them in one-on-one situations. You need help against Monroe and Gus and Unseld and the rest of them. And when you help out, you leave yourself vulnerable someplace else.

214

Even then Monroe can kill you. We tried everything on him in the first game. We tried to steer him into certain lanes. We double-teamed him. We had Frazier pressure him and tried to sneak Barnett in off the blind side. How did we make out? The Pearl got thirty-nine points.

Monroe was magnificent but we won in double overtime, so we were satisfied. We made some crucial plays when we needed them or else it would have been different. Baltimore had the opportunity for the last shot at the end of regulation and the first overtime but we escaped both times.

Each time, the Bullets isolated Monroe on Frazier. That was something to see. That was the real beauty of pro basketball right there. That was raw pressure. Imagine what Frazier and Monroe were going through—especially Monroe.

Here was The Pearl, in hostile territory, with most of the 19,500 Garden fans against him, handed the awesome responsibility of making the winning shot. The tension had to be unbelievable. But ballplayers like Monroe and Frazier are great because they have the ability to shut it all out. They know it is there but they don't. They were fighting nothing but each other. The clock, the people didn't mean a thing. The Pearl even forgot what time it was. He thought the end of regulation was the end of the third period.

Monroe came within an inch of beating us in regulation. His jumper from the top of the key hit the rim almost at the buzzer. He missed and the score remained tied at 102. The scoreboard clock was set at five minutes for the overtime period. The Pearl looked at it. "What's that five minutes doing up there?" he asked Frazier during the time out. Clyde explained it to him.

They spend a lot of time together in most ball games. Once in a while, I might change and put Barnett on Monroe to keep Frazier out of foul trouble. Sometimes Gene Shue will play Marin on Frazier to keep Monroe out of foul trouble. Frazier and Monroe are the kind of players who can hurt each other.

This time Monroe hurt us but didn't kill us. Baltimore had a good chance to win in the first overtime and Frazier saved it. The Bullets were leading, 110–108, and had the ball with about thirty seconds to go. It was Monroe and Frazier all by themselves near midcourt. We were trying to sneak Barnett over but The Pearl was too smart. He kept whirling away from trouble. Clyde somehow flicked out those fast hands and the ball was loose.

Barnett got the ball and was fouled and made two shots to tie it with twenty-three seconds remaining. Baltimore still had the advantage. The Bullets had the ball and a chance at the last shot once more. It looked like an instant replay of the previous play. Frazier knocked the ball loose again on Monroe and Barnett scooped it up.

I glanced at the clock. Five seconds. "All the way, all the way," I said more to myself than Barnett. He looked at the clock, too, so he knew he had time to lay it in. What no one took the time to consider was that any Baltimore player had a chance to stop Barnett.

Dick drove to the basket with the sure winner. He laid the ball against the board. So we thought, anyway, until Fred Carter came from out of nowhere and swatted the shot away. Carter is only 6-3 but can jump to the moon and he made the kind of play that coaches dream of. There was only one trouble from this coach's viewpoint—it was goaltending.

It looked to us that Carter had interfered with a shot that had hit the backboard, which is automatic goaltending in the NBA. We figured we had won. We were wrong. Mendy Rudolph, the senior official in the league and one

216

of the best ever, felt differently. He gave no signal for goaltending. He let time run out.

You can get a little upset about a call like that. It is easy to forget how good the referees really are when you think a mistake has been made on a winning shot. Mendy explained that Carter had caught the shot on its upward flight and cleanly knocked it away. He said the ball never touched the backboard.

When I look back, I see the whole incident from a different perspective. What I now remember is Carter. Players, coaches and referees have differences of opinions many times because pro basketball is the most impossible game to officiate. But how many times do you see a play such as the one Carter made. The speed, the hustle, the timing.

The game went into a second overtime tied at 110 and we won, 120–117, so now I can say Carter deserved the call, even if I disagreed. "I caught the ball with my hand before the ball hit the backboard," Fred insisted. "My hand hit it up. I knew Barnett had a step on me but I'm quicker than he is and I caught up with him."

That first game set the tone for the series. It went seven, and we won by taking the final game at home. There could never be a harder fought, better played, more exciting series. The Bullets and Knicks are well-matched teams. There is no dominating size or muscle on either side. There was no way either team could be overly confident or sure of anything.

We won the second game, and on Baltimore's floor, but we had no visions of repeating our sweep of the year before. We were coming back to the Garden for the third game and we knew Monroe and Johnson would cause trouble somehow. How did we know? We had just won a game where we were lucky, or just good enough.

I say good enough because Mike Riordan came off the bench and hit some big baskets and played some great defense. I say lucky enough because Bill Bradley took a key shot from the corner late in the game that hit the side of the board and bounced back to him and we scored, anyway. We won, 106–99, and could appreciate the frustration of the Bullets.

They hadn't beaten the Knicks in six straight playoff games. They had lost eleven in a row since beating Los Angeles in a 1965 playoff game. "I'm tired of this damn Mission Impossible script," said Marin disgustedly. It was disturbing.

I had sent Riordan in primarily for defense. Barnett had been playing Monroe and was tired. We were losing by six at the end of three quarters and Mike hit a couple of shots that got us the lead. Riordan seemed to surprise a lot of people for some reason. The newspapermen came in and wanted to know if I had any apprehension about putting a third guard into such a pressure situation.

If a coach has apprehension about a player, that player doesn't belong on the team, let alone in a game. "I haven't got any doubts about anyone on this ballclub," I said for the hundredth time. It still hurt the Bullets to lose that way.

"Two good ball games but they got them both," said Loughery. "For three-quarters we kicked the hell out of them," said Johnson. Well, not exactly. But they did lose two tough games and we knew they would be dangerous—more dangerous. They would be fighting for their lives now and that is what brings out the best in good ballplayers.

There was no doubt who won the third game. Baltimore got in front right away and stayed there. I played Barnett on Monroe again. I had changed after the first game to give The Pearl something else to think about. He had to concentrate on Barnett and also wonder where Frazier was lurking. This time The Pearl hit only ten of his eighteen shots and we *held* him to twenty-five points.

You had to hand it to the Bullets. They had to win this one or go home in a 3-0 hole. They had to do it in the Garden in front of all those screaming Knick fans. Don't ever underestimate the effect the home crowd has on a team. Both teams.

Let me tell you something. Those Knick fans can make noise. You sit on the floor, smack in the middle of it, and it explodes all around you. I realize that Mets fans and pro football fans can make a lot of noise but it's not the same thing. I'd say 19,500 people indoors can create a greater percussion than a hundred thousand or two hundred thousand in an outdoor stadium.

Every game that got us closer to the championship, the noise seemed to get louder. Eddie Layton, the Garden organist, figured the noise kept growing until he had boosted the decibel four times greater than when the season started. That's a lot of noise. When a visiting team can win under those conditions, it has won a ball game.

That is why coaches such as me keep saying we play them one at a time. How can you ever afford the luxury of looking past any game that has meaning. Take Loughery, for example. You wouldn't figure he would cause much trouble. His ribs still were tender and any blow in that area would be very painful.

But he was out there and he didn't even want to wear the protective brace because it restricted him. The doctors insisted and he wore it until the third game. Between the first and second periods, Kev told trainer Skip Feldman he couldn't stand it anymore. While his teammates stood around in the huddle, Loughery did a striptease and had the brace removed.

He wasn't concerned about anything but helping his team. He did. He played only ten minutes but at one time hit thirteen points that hurt us when we looked as though we were coming back. "I couldn't do a thing with that damned thing on," Loughery said of the five-pound brace. "I couldn't shoot and you get so damned sick and tired of the Knicks beating you. If we didn't win this one there wouldn't be much breath left in us."

Guys such as Loughery make the wheels go around. All teams have them. That is why no team can ever be sure. That is why we were not depressed or surprised that the Bullets won a game they had to win and on our court, no less. Unseld had a good game. He got thirty-four rebounds and we got thirty. Things like that confirm my suspicion that games are won more than they are lost.

We're not the best rebounding team in the world. Far from it. But imagine one player outrebounding our whole team—Reed and DeBusschere and everyone. Baltimore was capable of doing things like that on any given night. Frazier, a much better talker than I, explained the situation. "They're like a lion wounded in the grass," said Clyde after the Bullets cut our series lead to 2-1. "We'll have to go in there and kill them."

It didn't happen in the next game. The Bullets swarmed all over us from the start with a game that looked familiar. They picked us up all over the court and ran off to a big lead before we knew what happened. They played aggressive defense. They challenged us all over. Gus Johnson spilled the secret when it was over. "We beat them at their own game," said Gus after they won, 102–92. I knew I recognized it.

They even stole our crowd noise. There were 12,289 people in the Civic Center that night, but they sounded like 19,500 in Madison Square Garden. They screamed "We're Number One," and let us have it right between the eardrums. The Baltimore players said they had never seen such enthusiasm from their fans.

Well, our fans beat their fans in the next game and went ahead, 3-2. Reed's knee acted up again. The doctor gave him a shot to ease the pain. That's about all you can do for arthritis. Lucky thing it wasn't a horse race. The Bullets would have demanded a saliva test after Willis played forty-five minutes and got thirty-six rebounds and thirty-six points.

I kind of think Reed did react to some stimulant. He probably was upset by the thirty-four rebounds Unseld had gotten the night before. Emotion does play some small part in ball games but it can be overdone. I'm sure Unseld was just as emotional about the fifth game as Willis had been about the fourth.

When players like Unseld and Reed meet, they can't always do what they want to do. It happens sometimes. It happened in the fifth game and we won, 101–80. It was our best game of the series. It was Baltimore's worst. There was a connection in our minds. We liked to think our defense was somehow responsible for them missing 76 of their 104 shots and making only 3-for-30 in the second half.

"Tonight we didn't play their game or ours," said Gus Johnson. We played our game. A slight adjustment helped. Frazier went back to concentrating on hitting the open man and playing defense. He had been trying too hard to pick up the scoring when it dropped off in the third and fourth games. There is no way we can operate at maximum efficiency if each part doesn't function properly.

We needed only one more victory going back to Baltimore and the tension was building. You always tell yourself that you are used to it but the tension is there and you notice it. Bill Bradley, our man of letters, described it this way: "The intensity is there. It was there tonight and it will be there again. What wins the game is what you do on the floor. We went over our defense. We were a little more aggressive. Not reckless—bold."

I'm sure glad he went to Princeton and Oxford. He gave us great balance. No other team provided the newspapermen with such a diversity of expert analysts. Cazzie and Barnett on health foods. Reed on hunting and fishing. Frazier on styles and sleeping. Bradley on politics. DeBusschere on beer and the stock tables. Bowman on soul music. Riordan on short-order meals. Stallworth on hats. Hosket and May on Dayton. Warren on . . . on . . . Dammit! That Warren was so quiet, we never did find out on what he was an expert.

The sixth game was nerve-wracking for both teams as usual. After ten minutes we led 16–8. Some of our players felt they could have put it away if they had hit better while Baltimore was missing so much. I don't know. I wish everything was so simple. Maybe I don't. That would take all the fun out of life. Just think if everyone could figure out the winning horse. There'd be nothing to win.

You tell me how you can figure Reed's sixth game and then have him come up with ten points in forty-five minutes. He shot 2-for-14 and DeBusschere shot 2-for-11 and Bradley shot 1-for-9 and you know how they can shoot. Baltimore's defense was just better than ours that night. Our defense was tough but they were tougher.

They really won it in the third quarter. There was nothing we could do to stop Johnson and Monroe. Gus hit three in a row right at the start of the second half. He and The Pearl got twenty-eight of Baltimore's thirty points in the quarter and we never caught up.

I never saw our dressing room so quiet. There was no kidding or laughing. The newspapermen came in and chatted with the players. "It's good we're going home," said Frazier. "It means a lot emotionally," said DeBusschere. What meant the most to me was that the players

222

still were confident they weren't going to blow it all now. They had too much invested in the season.

I am sure Baltimore felt the same way, but it was at a slight disadvantage. The final game was in the Garden and I could just imagine the noise that was awaiting them. The fans had come up with a new chant: "Dee-fense! Dee-fense!" It's amazing how these things start. I wonder who thinks them up.

The Bullets had another problem. Monroe's knee was bothering him. He was suffering from wear and tear. They had to give him a cortisone shot in the dressing room after the sixth game. It had nothing to do with our plans. Anytime you play Baltimore you have to concern yourself with Earl and hope to accomplish two things: pressure him to give up the ball or try to make him take a bad percentage shot. The trouble is, he hits bad percentage shots as well as good ones.

Monroe got his thirty-two points though we played outstanding team defense. What more can I say about him. We got a great game out of everyone. This time it was Barnett who did the important scoring. Dick got thirteen baskets. More importantly, he played forty-one minutes of accelerated offense and defense. Monroe played him on defense and had a tough time.

"I was waiting for Barnett to get old," said Fred Carter. That about says it. A lot of ballplayers have gotten old waiting for Barnett to get old. "I'm a hero now," announced Dick as he was crushed by reporters and photographers after we won the seventh and deciding game, 127–114. "On this club it's not an individual thing. You got to subordinate things. I shot a little more than usual tonight."

We played the game the way it should be played. The players responded to every situation. Frazier harassed Monroe on defense and made him work hard, and that gave Barnett a little opening at the other end. DeBus-schere played a really aggressive game with thirteen re-bounds and twenty-eight points. Reed helped neutralize Unseld in one of their customary standoffs. Bradley made his contribution to team defense. And good old Cazzie came off the bench with seven baskets on fourteen shots when we needed them.

We were happy to see Baltimore go. Not that Milwau-kee looked any easier. The Bucks had eliminated Phila-delphia, 4-1, and a young man named Lew Alcindor had made life simply miserable for the 76ers. But we still were glad to see the last of the Bullets until next season—espe-cially Monroe. I laughed when I heard what Clyde had to say about The Pearl. So funny and so true.

"I'm tired of dreaming of that cat," said Frazier. "He's like a horror movie. It's a lot of sweat chasing him. He's such a great shooter. I say to myself: 'How can I stop him?'" I think we'll follow Loughery's advice from now on. "Use a gun," he suggested.

Now it was Alcindor, and Frazier had something to say about that. "One monster, now another," he said. That Clyde is so good with words, he ought to write a book someday. You know, every time I think of Alcindor I won-der if I wouldn't be better off as a writer, myself. He is some talent and he is only a youngster in the game.

Everyone on our team had a genuine respect for Alcin-dor and his teammates. Costello had done a nice job of building around him. Big Lew had made better players of everyone. That didn't mean he was the only player re-sponsible for taking Milwaukee from last place to second in one season. Flynn Robinson, Jon McGlocklin, Bob Dan-dridge, Greg Smith and Freddie Crawford had contributed their share.

Alcindor was great but there is no such thing as a one-man team. One man like Lew, Bill Russell, Walt Chamberlain or Nate Thurmond can be a tremendous influence but cannot win by himself. We think the Knicks proved that five are better than one. Yet there still were many people who looked on the New York-Milwaukee series as strictly between Reed and Alcindor.

Willis considered that nonsense. He told everybody he didn't go into a game against Baltimore thinking only of Unseld and he wasn't going into a series against Milwaukee thinking only of Alcindor. "I don't think I'll be doing anything like stopping Lew Alcindor," he explained. "We play team basketball. You just don't come out and try and stop one man."

He was not establishing an alibi in case Alcindor went wild. Reed is not like that. He is quite candid and honest about the things he says. "Lew's stretch is impossible," Willis said. "He's like a 747. With a guy like that, movement is important on offense so he doesn't stand in the middle and clog it. When he gets the ball, he's trying to move closer to the basket, so you got to establish your position. I don't know how much it will help."

Alcindor had been tough on us and everyone all season. He scored thirty-six, seventeen, twenty-six, twenty-five, forty-one and twenty-six in our regular season games. He didn't do badly in the playoffs, either. In the first game he got thirty-five points and fifteen rebounds; in the second, thirty-eight points and twenty-three rebounds; in the third, thirty-three points and thirty-one rebounds; in the fourth, thirty-eight points and nine rebounds; and in the fifth, twenty-seven points and eleven rebounds.

Milwaukee won only the third game—at home. If there was such a thing as the key game, it was the second. We won it by a point, 112–111. Alcindor missed two fouls when we were leading, 110–109, with fifty-two seconds to go. Cazzie made two, eighteen seconds later, that clinched it for us. That's the way it goes.

DeBusschere made a great play when he came from nowhere to block a sure basket by Crawford that would have put Milwaukee in front, 107–106. Cazzie came in and hit five straight shots. Alcindor played an incredible game but he is the one who felt the worst when it was over. He could hardly talk to anyone. He was thinking of those foul shots.

Alcindor had nothing to be ashamed of, but I could understand how he felt. He had done a masterful job and it had to end like that. We had collapsed all around him as in the first game, but this time he hit the open man for eleven assists. Who could ask for anything more? That is the cruel side of sports. Only the winners can enjoy winning.

Lew had his chance in the third game. We should have known something was wrong the way the stewardess greeted us on the plane. "Welcome to the World Champion Knickerbockers," she announced. "This is a nonstop charter to Cleveland." That was funny because we were going to Milwaukee. Maybe we should have gone to Cleveland.

The Bucks won, 101–96, and the fans out there went crazy. Alcindor got his points and rebounds, but the guy who hurt us most was Dandridge. He played forty-seven minutes and hit ten of his fifteen shots. That was their last victory. We took the next two, 117–105 and 132–96, and we were one giant step away from the first championship in the twenty-four-year history of the Knicks.

Organist Eddie Layton played: "California Here We Come." Only the Los Angeles Lakers stood in our way now. Only Wilt Chamberlain and Jerry West and Elgin Baylor. Only?

O
19

I rushed back into the house. "The muffler. Where's the muffler?" My family thought I had flipped my lid. A muffler on a very warm day late in April? Yes, a muffler on a very warm day late in April.

It was my lucky muffler. It had belonged to one of the newspapermen traveling with the Knicks. His mother-in-law had knitted it for him and I had borrowed it one cold night early in the season. I'm not really superstitious—only about a black, woolen muffler that coincided with an eighteen-game winning streak.

I wasn't without it then and I wasn't about to be without it now that the championship series was starting. I had worn it all season and I wore it when I left for the Garden and the first game with the Los Angeles Lakers. When you play against Wilt Chamberlain, Jerry West and Elgin Baylor, you need all the help you can get.

"West, Chamberlain and Baylor, that really adds up to something," was the way DeBusschere put it. Let's see: Chamberlain, someone figured, had 27,426 points entering the series; Baylor had 23,023 and West, 20,139. That added up to exactly 70,588 points for all their regular season and playoff appearances. Awesome.

Los Angeles, or Baylor and West, had a tremendous advantage over us in playoff experience. So did Chamberlain, who had been in many playoffs with other teams. The Lakers had been in the championship series six times in the last eight years. They never won because they had the misfortune of running into the Bill Russell era. This was the Knicks' first NBA final since they lost to the Lakers of Minneapolis in 1953.

We had taken the season series from the Lakers, 4-2, but Chamberlain had played in only one game. He was back and he was ready. He had started slowly in the first playoff with Phoenix and then got rolling against Atlanta. His knee wasn't perfect yet but he had recovered enough to be a dominating force, again, in any game.

Joe Mullaney said the Lakers never could have gotten to the championship round without Wilt, and who would know better. Yet, in due respect to Chamberlain, and I have a lot of respect for him, who could really say that Baylor and West wouldn't have made it, anyway. They had never gone all the way but they had been so close, so many times. They were exceptional pressure ballplayers, especially West.

He wants the ball in the clutch. He insists on it. He has a long history of winning baskets. He has the supreme confidence and exceptional talent that separates the superstar from the very good.

"Some players don't want the ball in the clutch. I do," West once said. "I want it bad. I just know I can make a basket. I have confidence because I've come through many times in the past. I'm not the only one. Far from it. I know I want the ball. I know the other players expect me to take it. I'm used to the responsibility. I'm used to tight situations. I enjoy them, I like the challenge."

Only Dick Barnett had been there before—when he was with the Lakers. But I was sure all the Knicks also liked a challenge. Both teams felt the same way. Each had come too far to lose. We had to control Chamberlain, West, Baylor and the others with our defense or it would be no contest. They had the size and scoring power. They had handled the rugged Atlanta Hawks, 4-0, and we always had trouble with Richie Guerin's team.

Wilt said it. "If they have any weakness," he pointed out, speaking of the Knicks, "it figures to be rebounding. The Knicks don't have any rebounding outside of Reed and DeBusschere. If we're gonna beat the Knicks, we're gonna have to outrebound them."

Chamberlain was partly right in theory but it didn't work out that way. The Lakers outrebounded us, 57-48, in the first game but we won, 124–112. Reed had a big game with thirty-seven points and sixteen rebounds. But you had to admire Wilt. He stayed out there for forty-eight minutes and grabbed twenty-four rebounds. Not bad at all for a guy they said would never make it back that season.

I think what helped us most was the way Reed shot from outside. Wilt gambled and gave Willis the outside to be in position for rebounds. "So what if Reed gets thirty or forty and we win," Chamberlain said before the game. "If he gets 'em inside, then I haven't done my job. If he's shooting twenty and twenty-five footers, and we get beat by them, I'll let him have them."

Reed hurt his shoulder jamming a shot and we were a little concerned about that. Mayor Lindsay dropped by and got Willis to laugh through his pain. The newspapers wrote mostly about how slow Chamberlain was reacting and how he had to be hurting to allow Mike Riordan and Cazzie Russell to drive all the way on him. I knew that would motivate Wilt when he read it.

"I'd like them to keep on driving," he said. It sounded ominous. I had to alert our players to be careful in the second game and be prepared to lay the ball off because Chamberlain would jam it down their throats. "We got bad reviews on Broadway," Wilt told his teammates. That also sounded ominous.

The doctor gave Reed something to ease the discomfort in his shoulder. Willis treated it as insignificant in view of Chamberlain's problems. "It takes a man with a lot of guts to come back and do what he is doing," Reed said of Wilt. "The guy played forty-eight minutes with a bad knee and nobody knows how bad it is except Wilt and he never alibis."

Reed went on about Chamberlain. "He proved that he can do whatever a team wants him to do—score, rebound, block shots and assists," said Willis. "He never had a chance to play with a group of players like Russell did. Only once and he proved he could do it in Philadelphia."

Wilt appreciated Willis's kind words and then went out and proved flattery will get you nowhere. He was much more active in the second game. He challenged Reed more and he dropped back to block off the inside when we tried to drive. The Lakers were more aggressive all around. They pressured us, just as we pressured them.

I think the big reason why they won the second game was that they got off in front. Chamberlain, West and Baylor are tough to chase. They know how to control a lead. It is rough enough trying to outscore them when you start even. Don't ever let them go right ahead, if you can help it. Who can help it?

We had many shots to win near the end but we lost, 105–103. Reed stole a pass with six seconds to go and we missed from the top of the key. We had a time-out left when Willis picked off the ball, and the writers wondered why I didn't use it and set up a play. A good question.

I explained that when Willis intercepted the pass, most of the Lakers were either downcourt or caught going the wrong way, so we wanted to exploit the advantage. I hope it was a good answer.

Wilt played forty-four minutes this time and again pulled in twenty-four rebounds. West played forty-six minutes and got thirty-four points, instead of thirty-three as in the opener. We went out to the Forum in Los Angeles tied, 1-1, and with nothing really established, other than that Wilt was not going to get caught flat-footed again, as in the first game.

The Forum is a nice place for a visiting team to play ball. The fans are not too noisy and they sit a little removed from the court. The place was designed by the same architect who designed the Garden except that he gave the Forum more of a Hollywood touch. Baylor supplies the dressing room with fried chicken from the place he owns. It would be a great place for a visiting team if it didn't have to worry about West or Chamberlain or Elgin.

I'll never forget what West did in the third game. Nobody will. That shot. What a shot! I couldn't believe it. You know, I went to a Los Angeles television station the next day to look at the video tape replay. I wanted to refresh my mind on the entire game, but I was mostly anxious to see the fifty-five-footer West threw in to send the game into overtime.

I sat there and saw Chamberlain toss the ball in and swore that he stepped onto the court too soon. I sat there and saw West heave the ball cleanly through the hoop with no seconds left and swore he ran two or three steps before the shot. It wasn't really that way. But I was looking for some reason to disprove that any human being could legitimately do what West had done to the Knicks.

I guess you just have to conclude that when West has the ball, he's just not human. We finally won the game in overtime, 111–108, but that West shot was unreal. I saw DeBusschere drop to the floor under our basket when the ball went through and I felt the same way. We all did. No one could talk. For the first time, even I had trouble finding my voice.

Imagine ninety-two feet away with three seconds to go. A pass-in from Chamberlain, a few strides by West and then a one-hand push right through from beyond midcourt. DeBusschere had just put us ahead, 102–100. No wonder Dave almost fainted. "My heart sunk. I was dumfounded," he said. "It's the longest clutch shot I've ever seen. I was directly under the basket and my heart dropped into my stomach. It just deflated me and I actually collapsed to the floor and my mind went blank. Clyde and I just stared at each other."

It was not exactly uncontested, either. Reed was right there with West. He was careful not to foul Jerry. He just wanted to distract him. Not that Willis thought it mattered. Who could make a shot like that from there? West did and thank goodness, for those who think they saw it, he explained how it happened.

"I was trying to get in the middle of the court a little bit and Willis picked me up and forced me across," he said. "When I let it go, it looked good. It was straight enough and far enough. My body was behind it and I was up in the air. I was just about at the top of the key—just about a step from there. I took off from there and when I hit, I covered about six or eight feet more."

He sure stunned everyone, especially us. I had to call the players off the floor to remind them the game was only tied. Frazier just stood there, staring into space. I suggested in the huddle that we forget it and think about the next five minutes. We did. It was a shame that West had to lose after a shot like that. It would have been a

232

shame if we had lost after the way DeBusschere and Barnett and all our guys had played.

By all rights, that game should have ripped the Lakers deep in their guts. They also came out of it with West's left thumb badly bruised and swollen. They said he might not play the fourth game. We had our own troubles. Reed's left knee was bad—very bad. He was limping around the motel the afternoon of the game.

Danny Whelan worked on him. Danny used heat and massages. Willis said he could play. I was prepared to use Bowman if Reed felt the knee hurt too much. Willis pushed himself for fifty-two minutes in the fourth game because that one also went into overtime. He limped a lot. The Lakers won this time, 121–115, sending the series back to New York and Madison Square Garden, tied once more, 2-2.

West, bad thumb and all, got thirty-seven points and was credited with eighteen assists. Reed, bad knee and all, got twenty-three points and twelve rebounds. Frazier said it about West but could have said it just as easily about Willis. "If he had a broken leg," Clyde pointed out, "he would've played. This means a lot to him. He's a pro; he has a lot of pride. I think it helped psych them up. That team without West would be through. They'd be hurting."

Yes, they could say the same thing about Reed and the Knicks, and they did pretty soon. In the next three games, or in two at least, Willis and the Knicks were to prove they were extraordinary. When we headed home for the fifth game, we were worried about Reed's knee. We sent him to the doctor and he prescribed ultrasonic and whirlpool. Willis had a standard answer when anyone asked how he felt. "I'm alright," he'd say.

He said it in the dressing room after the fourth game and he flinched when a reporter pointed at the swelling.

"Don't touch it," Reed begged the writer. But Willis insisted he could play when we discussed it before the fifth game. I don't accept the word of a player in a case like that. It is up to the doctor and he said Willis could play.

Willis played. Not for long. Only eight minutes. He started to drive left on Chamberlain and down he went. The ball popped from underneath Reed and Wilt picked it up and started the play going the other way.

Reed remained stretched out on his right side. He clutched his right hip. He turned over and sat up. He put his head in his arm. He was in pain. Danny Whelan and I ran out. We thought it was his knee. It turned out to be a torn muscle near the hip bone. Willis and Whelan went to the dressing room with Dr. James Parkes, who was pinch-hitting for Dr. Andrew Patterson, our team physician.

The game went on. I sent Bowman in against Chamberlain. Then Hosket. When Willis left, we were losing by ten points. It got to thirteen at intermission when we left to see how Reed was. We found out we would have to play without him. Willis wanted to get back in but couldn't lift his leg.

He was stretched out on the trainer's table when I walked in and got the news from Dr. Parkes. I went into the dressing room to tell the players. They had heard. They were disappointed but not beaten. We discussed what we would do without Reed at center. Bradley came up with an idea. He suggested we use a 1-3-1 offense because the Lakers were using a zone defense. We needed something to get open shots and Bill had made a sound suggestion.

Frazier was the outside man. Bradley was at the top of the key. Cazzie and Barnett roamed the sides and De-Busschere, opening at center, ran the baseline. Later we used Stallworth against Wilt and got even more motion.

234

It worked beautifully and convinced me even more that a coach is a fool if he does not encourage ideas from his players.

Before we went out for the second half, the players went into the trainer's room to see Willis. They told him they were going to win it for him. "You big sissy, you," Clyde said to Reed. "We ain't gonna let you be captain anymore. But when you come back, you'll be captain, won't you?"

I think we won the championship right there in that second half without Willis. If Los Angeles had won that fifth game, it would have been all over in the sixth out there. We did it with the help of Bradley's suggestion and the perfect application of it by the players. As a coach, I can assure you any idea is as good as the players carry it out.

The Knicks had an unusual bunch of players. They were not crushed by the loss of Reed. They had complete faith in themselves as a team and as much as Willis meant, they still felt they were a team. "I thought we could do it with what we had on the floor," explained Bradley. "I just wasn't talking about the five that start, but the whole team. It's a difficult concept to get across to people."

We attacked the Laker defense at one end and harassed them at the other. We set up our defense to try to keep Wilt from getting the ball because of the tremendous advantage he had on DeBusschere and Stallworth. That is what *we* tried to do. I am in no position to explain what Los Angeles tried to do.

What happened was gratifying to me and disappointing to Mullaney. The Lakers got only twenty-six shots in the second half. West took two shots, Wilt three. It was incredible. Our defense was incredible. We swarmed all over the ball handler and still seemed to have someone in position to deflect a pass intended for Chamberlain. We cut it to 82–75 by the fourth quarter and we passed them when Bradley hit a shot from the corner to make it 93–91. We had trailed for forty-one minutes and nineteen seconds.

We had no time to think of Reed by then but he was tuned in to us. He was sitting in the dressing room and listening to the play-by-play being piped in to him by Johnny Condon, the public address announcer. Condon would make like a commentator into a special phone that is connected to our room and then cut away to his microphone to inform the crowd about baskets and fouls.

It was tricky but Reed got it all as we pulled away in the closing minutes to win, 107–100, to take a 3-2 lead in the series. "Unbelievable. Goddam!" yelled Reed as Condon shrieked over the phone: "It's gonna be all over. Frazier steals again. Frazier's shot is good." It was all over.

We ran to the dressing room. Reed was standing near his stool. The players went at him, screaming. They hammered him. Cazzie kissed him. "We did it for you, big fella," said Caz. What a victory! The kind you remember all your life. Every detail.

Tomorrow always comes around and you have to go on. We had to leave for Los Angeles and we took Willis with us. We had a day in between before the next game and we figured we might get Reed ready. Dr. Parkes came along. "The longest house call in history," someone called it.

Dr. Parkes took Willis to a health club for the sauna. He used ultrasonic and whirlpool and massages. No good. We were looking for a medical miracle and didn't get it. Willis sat on the bench in civilian clothes the next night and saw the Lakers win, 135–113, and send the series back to New York for the seventh and deciding game.

Chamberlain and West just destroyed us. Wilt got forty-five points and twenty-seven rebounds, Jerry thirty-three points and thirteen assists. Willis kept coaching Bowman to brace himself against Chamberlain and try to keep him from muscling in. We didn't get away with smaller centers that night. "Wilt made up his mind to go to the hoop and what good is a little guy, even Bowman," said DeBusschere. "We needed a strong guy like Willis to stop him. That was the difference tonight."

Not exactly. The Lakers got the ball to Wilt more and that is why he was able to go to the hoop. They set the rhythm and there was nothing we could do about it. Now we had to concern ourselves with the seventh game. We had to have Reed if he was able to walk at all. Everyone knew that.

I also knew something else. There was no way I would let him play if the doctor indicated he might suffer a permanent injury. Championship or no championship. We were going to try our best to get him ready if we could. We arranged for Willis to leave for New York right after the game at the Forum. We wanted him to use as much of the remaining forty-eight hours or so for whatever treatment he needed.

"If he gives us half a game, we'll win," said DeBusschere. "Willis on one leg is better than anyone we have." We sent Danny Whelan back with Willis. They flew to New York while we were sleeping. They landed at Kennedy airport at 6:45 New York time and arrived at the Garden around 7:30, which was just about the time we were leaving Los Angeles.

Whelan has a funny way of describing things. "It was so early, the pigeons were on the sidewalk having their breakfast," he explained. "When they saw Willis, they got frightened and scattered." Danny went to work on Willis right away. There was whirlpool and massage and hot packs and ultrasonic for about three hours. Reed then went home to rest.

The next day, the day of the game, Willis went to see Dr. Parkes for a progress report. It was decided to keep up the treatments and then have Willis suit up and test his leg. He had a muscle tear and it was painful but he insisted he would play. "The worst I can do is hurt it," he said, "but I've played in pain before." It still would be up to Dr. Parkes and he wanted to wait until Willis worked out.

We sent Reed out to the court around six o'clock. The doctor watched, I watched. Chamberlain watched. Willis took some shots and moved a little. He said he felt alright. We went back to the dressing room and we talked again. Reed said he could play, and it was decided to let him. The doctor would give him a shot to ease the pain just before he went on the floor.

It was obvious that Reed could not run or jump, so we had to make that part of it easy for him. All we wanted from him was to lean on Wilt and keep him from rolling to the basket. (That's all?) I told Willis to forget about running hard on defense. I told him to lay back when the Lakers were shooting fouls—not line up along the lane.

That way he could save all his strength for Chamberlain and minimize the chances of aggravating his injury. There was a lot of tension in the dressing room. I think I gave them my customary send-off: "This is a big game." I wasn't really thinking of them. I had Willis Reed on my mind. So did everyone.

I went into the trainer's room. Willis was there with Dr. Parkes. The doctor was waiting to the last second to inject Reed. I later found out it was carbocaine and cortisone. I also learned the medical terms for his injury—he had torn the rectus femoris and tensor muscles, whatever they are. It was about 7:25, or some ten minutes before game time when Dr. Parkes took out a six-inch needle and jabbed it into Willis' right thigh.

238

By then, the players on both sides had their warm-ups and were about ready to start the game. The fans were chanting "We want Willis." Reed left the dressing room with enough time to get a few shots. There was a tremendous roar when the fans saw him. All the players stopped and looked around. Even the Los Angeles players.

Reed was limping and we were asking a lot of him to try to neutralize Chamberlain. That is all we had in mind. We were not thinking of psyching or anything like it. We needed Willis in there at the start because no one can let the Lakers get away fast. We had to keep Wilt and West from breaking it open right away. We expected nothing more from Willis than to prevent Wilt from getting the ball where he could murder us.

We got much more than we expected. Reed, dragging his leg and trailing every offensive play, hit his first two shots. Wilt gave him plenty of room. Willis popped one from the side and one from the head of the key and the 19,500 Garden fans went crazy. So did the Knicks. That is all we seemed to need.

Willis played twenty-one minutes in the first half and Wilt got eleven shots, most of them going away from the hoop. We accelerated the game once Reed gave us the lift-off. DeBusschere, Bradley, Barnett and Frazier just flew all over the place. There was only one traumatic moment. Reed went up for a Chamberlain miss and DeBusschere barrelled into him.

The captain went down in pain. Willis insisted he could keep playing. He limped back into the game and the fans cheered. It was his night. We kept him in the dressing room at half time until the last minute because he wanted another shot. The pain was excruciating but Willis told Dr. Parkes to give him some more of that stuff, whatever it was. Reed hates needles but he wasn't going to let that stand in his way at that time.

Both teams were lined up for the center jump when Willis came shuffling out of the runway. The fans spotted him and the noise must have disturbed seismographs all over the country. Bowman was out there on the court but I signaled Mendy Rudolph if it was okay to send in Reed. He nodded. I waved to Willis and he made a short left from the baseline and trotted onto the floor.

It was very dramatic. There were some people who accused me of staging the whole thing—Willis's late entry before the game and at the start of the second half. They figured I was trying to psych the Knicks and the Lakers. I wish I could say I was that smart. I guess as the years go on, I'll probably say I did it deliberately. It'll sound good to my grandchildren, anyway.

Willis only played six minutes in the second half. We didn't need him. He had done the job in the first half when we built a 69–42 lead. The others took it from there. Barnett, Frazier, DeBusschere and Bradley weren't about to let it go. Reed sat on the bench near me as the minutes and the seconds ticked away.

It is hard to describe the feeling as you sit and watch the clock moving you closer to a championship. All those years, all those games, and now the Knicks were about to win it all for the first time. Reed and I talked to each other, but neither had any idea what we were saying. We heard the fans chanting: "We're Number One!" We saw the scoreboard clock approaching triple zero—the final stop on the merry-go-round.

It arrived. We scrambled for the dressing room. We were champions. The Knicks were beautiful. The world was beautiful. "I feel like crying," said rookie John Warren.

Index

241

242

243

245